This is not just another good book about surviving a suicide. It's actually a book about life and hope and new beginnings. Rita writes with the compassion of a survivor and the wisdom of a therapist. She doesn't minimize the pain. She addresses the difficult issues head-on. It's realistic and faith-affirming. I so wish that I'd had this resource when I lost a young adult son to suicide. This is a book that you will want to read more than once.

Gary Oliver, ThM, PhD
Licensed Clinical Psychologist; Executive Director, The Center for Healthy Relationships; Professor of Psychology & Practical Theology, John Brown University

Surviving Suicide Loss is a valuable contribution to suicide literature and a gift to the survivor community. Written with wisdom and grace, the book offers solid support for those grappling with the profound grief that follows the suicide of a loved one. Schulte writes beautifully, and she has shared her story in a way that will make a difference for others who are grieving a suicide. Information and helpful suggestions, along with kindness and compassion permeate every sentence of this book. Reading it was like talking with a friend who understands suicide grief completely—because they have traveled that same journey.

Ronnie Susan Walker MS, LCPC
Founder & Executive Director, Alliance of Hope for Suicide Loss Survivors

Too many books of this type are strictly personal accounts of survival or an impersonal self-help guide. This is different. Not only does Schulte write about her own journey after her husband's suicide, but she offers an amazing amount of helpful advice in poignant, caring language. I was especially impressed with the practical challenges in her "Consider This" at the end of each chapter. Although every chapter is impressive, the one I rarely see much written about is chapter 9, "Making Peace with Ourselves."

Cecil Murphey
Author or coauthor of 140 books, including bestsellers such as *Gifted Hands: The Ben Carson Story* and *90 Minutes in Heaven*

W9-AFI-167

Deaths by suicide are catastrophes, and the bereaved are left behind to face a lifetime of sometimes unanswerable "why" questions and the possibility of a shattered belief system, among other woes. In this book, Rita Schulte provides the dual insight of both clinician and suicide loss survivor, giving the reader a roadmap through the darkness that can overtake survivors. With numerous exercises and practical teaching for healing, this book will be an excellent resource to help survivors create new sustainable frameworks of meaning in areas of life challenged by a suicide loss.

DR. THOMAS JOINER
The Robert O. Lawton Distinguished Professor of Psychology, Florida State University

There is no word by itself that triggers more alarm, fear, and pain than suicide. Its impact shakes families, schools, churches, and communities. In her latest book, *Surviving Suicide Loss*, Rita takes us on a rare journey on how to process and work through one of life's most difficult situations. In sharing her story, Rita helps bring clarity, comfort, and peace to those who have been deeply impacted by suicide. Rita's words remind us that in the midst of great tragedy and loss, there is hope found in Christ.

DR. TIM CLINTON
President of the American Association of Christian Counselors

Brutally honest . . . poignantly helpful, not a casually written book, but rather profound from page to page. Rita is "real" before us, and wise with her words. To help you heal, heed her call to "make room for spiritual growth"—she even helps us with the how.

JUNE HUNT
Founder, CEO, CSO (Chief Servant Officer), Hope For The Heart; author, *Counseling Through Your Bible Handbook*

SURVIVING SUICIDE LOSS

—

MAKING YOUR
WAY BEYOND *the* RUINS

—

RITA A.
SCHULTE, LPC

NORTHFIELD PUBLISHING

CHICAGO

All Scripture quotations, unless otherwise indicated, are taken from the Holy Bible, New International Version®, NIV®. Copyright © 1973, 1978, 1984, 2011 by Biblica, Inc.™ Used by permission of Zondervan. All rights reserved worldwide. www.zondervan.com The "NIV" and "New International Version" are trademarks registered in the United States Patent and Trademark Office by Biblica, Inc.™

Scripture quotations marked TLB are taken from The Living Bible copyright © 1971 by Tyndale House Foundation. Used by permission of Tyndale House Publishers Inc., Carol Stream, Illinois 60188. All rights reserved. The Living Bible, TLB, and the The Living Bible logo are registered trademarks of Tyndale House Publishers.

Scripture quotations marked ISV are taken from the The Holy Bible: International Standard Version. Release 2.0, Build 2015.02.09. Copyright © 1995–2014 by ISV Foundation. ALL RIGHTS RESERVED INTERNATIONALLY. Used by permission of Davidson Press, LLC.

All emphasis in Scripture has been added.

Names and details of some stories have been changed and others are composites to protect the privacy of individuals.

Published in association with the literary agency of Hartline Literary, 123 Queenston Drive, Pittsburgh, PA 15235.

Edited by Amanda Cleary Eastep
Interior Design: Ragont Design
Cover Design: Connie Gabbert Design
Cover image of path copyright © 2019 by Milosz Aniol / Shutterstock (396940942). All rights reserved.

Library of Congress Cataloging-in-Publication Data

Names: Schulte, Rita A., author.
Title: Surviving suicide loss : making your way beyond the ruins / Rita A. Schulte.
Description: Chicago : Northfield Publishing, 2021. | Includes bibliographical references. | Summary: "If you are struggling with suicide loss or you need to come alongside someone who is, Rita Schulte wants to help. As a suicide loss survivor, she understands the pain because she has been there too. Her science-based therapy model that takes human spirituality into account offers hope"-- Provided by publisher.
Identifiers: LCCN 2021014630 (print) | LCCN 2021014631 (ebook) | ISBN 9780802420985 (paperback) | ISBN 9780802499103 (ebook)
Subjects: LCSH: Loss (Psychology) | Grief. | Suicide. | Psychic trauma. | Counseling--Religious aspects--Christianity.
Classification: LCC BF575.D35 S368 2021 (print) | LCC BF575.D35 (ebook) | DDC 155.9/37--dc23
LC record available at https://lccn.loc.gov/2021014630
LC ebook record available at https://lccn.loc.gov/2021014631

We hope you enjoy this book from Northfield Publishing. Our goal is to provide high-quality, thought-provoking books and products that connect truth to your real needs and challenges. For more information on other books and products that will help you with all your important relationships, go to www.northfieldpublishing.com or write to:

Northfield Publishing
820 N. LaSalle Boulevard
Chicago, IL 60610

1 3 5 7 9 10 8 6 4 2

Printed in the United States of America

Mike—safely home

"When darkness overtakes him, light will come bursting in."
Psalm 112:4 TLB

Contents

Author's Note

I'd like to first acknowledge my husband, Michael William Schulte. Strange, I know, since this book is about his death by suicide, but I wanted to take a moment and acknowledge his *life*. In the pages that follow, you will hear about my husband's illness and death by suicide; but that *isn't* his story. The real story is a story of faith, hope, and love. It's about how he touched people's lives and brought hope and healing to them, not only through his dental office, but through his just being who he was. He was a good man. A loving man. A very generous man. A man who loved God with a passion and who loved his family and friends. He used his gifting as a dentist to minister to those who were less fortunate, and in his practice, which at times seemed more like my counseling office, he prayed with the weary and brokenhearted, pointing them to God.

Mike was an activist. He was an advocate for the unborn, and he spent years of his life giving time and attention to that work. He was involved in missions in Nicaragua where he ministered to the poor, helped build homes, and supported an orphanage. He was everyone's hero, but as we sometimes see in tragedies, heroes can often fall. Mike Schulte left a big legacy, and his untimely death left an even bigger hole.

And that's what this book is about: helping you, who are left behind after your own loss due to suicide, climb out of that black hole and make your way beyond the ruins.

Introduction

It seems like yesterday, and yet it seems like a million years ago. Each anniversary is a marker, reminding me I've lived another year without a part of my soul. I should be completely better after all this time, right? At least that's what my Western culture tells me; and yet at times, I still feel displaced. Shattered. Alone.

The toxic thoughts and bodily sensations so reminiscent of Post-Traumatic Stress Disorder (PTSD) still revisit me on occasion. Picturing myself huddled in a corner shaking or curled up in a ball in the weeks and months after finding my husband had died by suicide is an all-too-familiar body memory that became commonplace the first year and a half. Flashbacks of the trauma accompanied by feelings of helplessness and terror made me despair of my own life. And then there's the guilt, the monster that can paralyze me when I least expect it, threatening to swallow me alive. This is the face of trauma, and it's for this reason that I wanted to write this book: to help you, my fellow survivor, navigate through the dual process of both grief and traumatic loss after a suicide.

As a survivor, I've spent the last several years trying to climb out of a black hole. Where did the years go, and how could I have survived them without Mike? He was my life. I've often felt like the Tin Man, alive with no heart. I suppose that is to be expected after forty-three years with someone. I honestly believe I wouldn't still be standing if it wasn't for my faith and the host of beloved friends and family who walked alongside me as I tried to make meaning out of this senseless tragedy.

If you've picked up this book, I know you understand. If you're a survivor of suicide loss (meaning you have lost someone to a death by suicide), or if you want to walk alongside someone who has lost a loved one to suicide, this book is for you. As someone who has walked this dark night of the soul before you, this is what I want you to know: don't give up. Don't *ever* give up. I know you want to. I did too. Life without Mike was unimaginable. I didn't believe I could bear the anguish of living in a world without him, much less navigate through something so traumatizing as a death by suicide. I knew life would never be the same. I was terrified.

As survivors of a loved one's suicide, we have experienced a *traumatic* loss. Post-traumatic stress is applicable to anyone who is confronted with a situation that is physically or emotionally beyond their ability to cope. In other words, the shock of the experience overwhelms the brain's ability to process what has been seen or experienced.

Here's the good news: with help, time, and others committed to walking alongside me, I began to live again. I want to show *you* the resources, tools, and support that are necessary so that you can live again too. You can't go this journey alone and get better. If you're suffering from prolonged depression, symptoms of post-traumatic stress, including severe anxiety, nightmares, or flashbacks, or if you can't eat or sleep, I encourage you to seek out a professional counselor who specializes in trauma. Use this book as an adjunct, not as a substitute for professional counseling.

Throughout the book, I'll be sharing parts of my story with you. Stories are meant to be told and shared for a couple reasons: first, so that others may benefit from the wisdom we have gleaned along our journey, and second, because there is healing in the telling. The secrets we keep and the lies we believe will only grow deeper roots in our souls with silence. This doesn't mean you need to share your story with everyone, but I believe you need to find a couple of safe people to walk alongside you through this journey as a survivor.

The approach of this book will be holistic, meaning it will address body, soul, and spirit. It will present teaching and interventions accordingly. Grief work is gut-wrenching. It drains every part of your being. I want to optimize your physical health so that, together, we can tackle this difficult work. Again, this book is *not* meant to take the place of professional counseling; it's meant to be used as an additional resource.

I'll be teaching you techniques to calm your overactive nervous system and ground you to the present. You'll learn how to breathe, how to focus, and how to pay attention to what you're trying to pay attention to. Many folks, including me, have a genetic propensity toward anxiety; trauma only adds fuel to that fire. If you have gone through a traumatic loss, it's not unusual to get immobilized by these emotions. Anxiety puts us in a continual state of activation, which leads to all kinds of stress-related health issues. Therefore, the skills you'll learn in these first few chapters about the brain, mindful noticing, and relaxation will be the foundation for all the other work we will do.

We will also look at spirituality. Research has shown that this is a vital part of recovery through grief and related trauma, and spiritual practice has gained plenty of momentum over the past decade. As a Christian, I can tell you that God showed up for me in so many amazing ways throughout this journey, and that's what ultimately got me through.

I believe suffering and tragedy can do one of two things in our lives: propel us toward hope or lead us to despair. That hope can lead us to a deeper spiritual walk. The lack of it can make us turn away from God altogether. Whatever your faith base, your spirit is core to your being. To heal from such a traumatic loss, you must make room for spiritual growth and understand where your true identity lies.

I chose to call this book *Surviving Suicide Loss: Making Your Way Beyond the Ruins* because through the power of presence, I was able to make my way beyond the ruins I was left with in my life. I got better. Now I want to walk with you through this most difficult journey and teach others how to do the same. So does God. That may be hard to hear now because you may be angry with God. I understand. Just take what you can use from this book and leave the rest till you're ready. What worked for me may not work for you, but I'll give you lots of options, and if even if one thing helps you, I'll have done my job.

Although I won't know each of you who may read this book, we are inextricably linked together through what has happened to us. I hope that makes you feel a little less alone. My prayer is that because I have gone before you, I can provide encouragement, hope, and some skills that may ease your agony as you struggle to make your way out of the darkness.

Chapter 1

Fallout

"My days have passed; my plans have been shattered;
along with my heart's desires."
—Job 11:17 ISV

I don't remember much of what happened. I remember the blood. I remember my husband's white T-shirt. I remember hearing myself screaming, running down the hallway, and curling up in a ball downstairs on the kitchen floor. Somehow, I managed to call my son. To this day, I'm stunned I could even remember his number. The phone rang and my daughter-in-law, Ida, answered as I shrieked and sobbed into the phone that Mike had killed himself. I was hysterical.

I could hear my son Michael in the background begin to scream and wail as he heard the conversation. Ida told me to call 911 but then immediately realized I wasn't capable. She said she would do it and for me to go and sit by the side door and wait till the police arrived. I don't remember how I got to the side door, but I was curled up in a ball shaking when the officer arrived. Then everything went blank.

My name is Rita Schulte. I'm a licensed psychotherapist in Northern Virginia. I spend my time helping people who are struggling with all types of mental health disorders: anxiety, depression, grief/loss, and eating disorders. Many of them go on to live happy and productive lives, but most tragically, I couldn't help one—my beloved husband, Mike. On November 12, 2013, after three short months of being severely depressed, anxious, and extremely paranoid, he shot himself in our bed, and I walked in to find him.

Traumatic moments like this shatter the soul. The impact of my discovery that fateful November afternoon created scars that will forever be etched upon my heart. In a split second, one shot changes your entire life. Nothing is ever the same after someone dies by suicide. As Anne-Grace Scheinin says, "Suicide doesn't end the pain. It only lays it on the broken shoulders of survivors."[1] It would be a very long and dark journey back—for all of us.

As people began to pour in that evening, shock and numbness clothed me like a heavy blanket. I remember nothing except a few questions the police officer asked me. I remember my daughter Ashley coming in crying and wanting to go upstairs to see her dad, and the officers told her no way. She couldn't believe it was true. No one could. Mike was Superman. Everyone loved him. Everyone leaned on him. But even Superman needed help. Unfortunately, he refused it until it was too late.

LEFT BEHIND

The fallout from any traumatic event can be cataclysmic, as any survivor knows. It seems like a lifetime of years since I lost Mike, and I still can't fit all the puzzle pieces back together. Some days, I often feel as if I'm falling backwards. Mike and I were high school sweethearts. I was sixteen when we met. We married at twenty-one and had forty-three years together. It wasn't all easy, as any couple knows, but it was an amazing ride, and he was an amazing man.

Mike had talked of suicide a number of times beginning in May of 2013. He started exhibiting symptoms of extreme paranoia by August. He believed everyone was after him, and at one point, that included me. He made several attempts during a three-month period, but something always stopped him. His doctor even told me that he believed Mike wanted to live.

My kids and I never believed Mike would really take his life. He always had a tendency toward the dramatic to drive a point home;

but one night, after coming home from work, I went into the sun-room to finish some work only to hear gunshots coming from our back field. I went screaming through the house trying to find Mike, finally ending up outside as my son pulled up the driveway. I fell to the ground screaming and shaking as I saw Mike come walking down from the field toward us with a gun in his hand.

Another day, he kissed me goodbye and left for work at his dental office, only he never got there. I got a call saying he never showed up for work. Patients were waiting. Once again, I called our son, and he came right over to get me. Mike was a dentist as well as an airplane pilot. He kept his plane in a hangar about twenty minutes away from our home. I just had a gut feeling to go there.

We didn't have the key to the hangar, and after much effort we located someone to open it for us. I sat in the car frozen and immo-bilized as my son went in. I couldn't feel my arms. When Michael didn't come right out, I started yelling for him. Michael responded: "Mom, he's in here!" It was over one hundred degrees in the hangar, and Mike had been in there in his parked car for hours.

Mike had an old photo of us from high school on the console. When Michael got him out of the car, Mike was totally dissociated. Dissociation is not simply a wandering mind or daydreaming; dis-sociative states usually accompany mental health disorders and are out of the individual's control. Their minds literally cannot process information correctly.

When I saw Mike, I fell to the ground clutching his legs and crying hysterically with relief. I immediately called his psychiatrist and took him to the ER. By the time we got there, he was laughing and joking like nothing was wrong! He told me not to mention any-thing about suicide because of the dental practice. I couldn't totally comply with his wishes.

Mike refused treatment. I believe he was afraid. Sometimes he would just shake and cry. It was gut-wrenching seeing him like that. He wouldn't take the medication that was prescribed. He wouldn't agree to go to a treatment center—until one day I got really mad at him. I think he believed nothing could help him. My son told me his dad had said he was only agreeing to go for me.

One night lying in bed, Mike told me he could never really take his life because he could never be without me, and he would never leave me with all the mess that would be left behind. My mistake was believing him. This only fueled my guilt: I mean, I was the counselor, right? Yet, I couldn't save my own husband from taking his life. I was drowning in guilt. Perhaps you can relate.

I am no stranger to grief and loss. I have weathered my children getting struck by lightning in a parasailing accident, falling twenty stories from the sky, and being badly burned. I have had both my beloved parents die in my arms after caring for each of them in our home. I have lost dear friends and family; but the fallout from discovering my husband shot to death in our bed was unimaginable. All I kept telling everyone in those early days was, *I'm not going to be able to make it through this. I will never be able to get over this!*

Finding a loved one who has died by suicide adds another layer to the traumatic event. Thirty years prior to my husband's death, Mike's sister's husband took his life, so suicide was not unfamiliar to our family. My sister-in-law didn't find her husband but was tormented about his final moments and replayed images over and over in her mind. Either way, the tapes don't stop. It's like the mind is stuck imagining the horror of the scene.

Warring against suicide is obviously a very personal fight for me. We need to carefully assess and treat those individuals who are struggling with suicidal thoughts or behaviors, and we need to do everything we can to destigmatize mental illness. Each year we hear of celebrities and high-profile people who lose their lives to suicide. Thousands have gone before them and will follow if we don't continue to address this issue. Suicide and opiate addiction have actually lowered life expectancy in the United States and the World Health Organization estimates that depression will become a leading cause of death if something isn't done to heighten awareness and improve treatment.[2]

Destigmatizing mental illness will do a couple things: first, it will help those who are struggling feel safe enough to actually *share* their struggles. Mike, as countless others do, hid his clinical issues because of one thing—*shame*; and the more we hide, the more shame grows. Second, talking openly and educating others about mental health issues will bring knowledge and understanding so that individuals who are struggling will not feel like second-class citizens.

This stigma unfortunately affects survivors as well. We have all become part of a group we would never have chosen—suicide loss survivor—and because others don't know what to do or say to us, we are often left feeling isolated and alone. As we will see in a later chapter, the fallout from a death by suicide leads the survivor to experience what therapists call "complicated grief."

Suicide is not a normal anticipated manner of death. We generally anticipate someone dying of a disease, in an accident, or of old age. Stigma surrounds suicide, so we as survivors are left to bear not only the loss and trauma, but also the mystery, the whispers, the insensitive comments, and all the questions that follow. Only, we have no concrete answers, no real explanations and no real closure.

My heart for all of us who have been left behind is that people honor the silent scream of our souls and don't expect us to "get over it" in a few months, or even a few years. We will *never* get over it. We just find a place to put it, and we do that with much greater ease when people who love us are patient, present, and emotionally available for us; when they listen and don't judge; and when they sit with us for as long as is necessary as we try to make meaning out of such a senseless tragedy.

WHY?!

I show a clip in my workshops from the movie *Secret in Their Eyes*.[3] It stars Julia Roberts and Nicole Kidman. There's a horrific scene in the movie where Roberts discovers the body of her dead daughter. The shock, horror, and agony of her discovery accurately depict the face of trauma. Her cry is the cry of despair. It was my cry. Maybe it's been your cry. We may not scream; we may not wail. We may be silent or become numb and unable to speak. It's all normal in light of what has happened.

This cry of despair is what trauma survivors live with every single moment of every single day. Unbearable anguish. So, before we can talk about moving forward, or post-traumatic growth (PTG, as we therapists like to call it), we must first honor the shattering. The Bible eloquently depicts what trauma survivors are left with in this verse from the book of Job, chapter 17, verse 11 (isv): "My days have passed; my plans are shattered; along with my heart's desires." The shattering gives way to the whys?! They are are the silent scream of the soul. Here are a few that we as survivors struggle with:

Why is this happening to me?

After I discovered that my husband had shot himself, I ran screaming from our room and downstairs to the kitchen where I collapsed onto the floor. I immediately curled up in a ball and began shaking. Because trauma overwhelms the brain's ability to process that kind of information, and the part of the brain that controls language shuts down, survivors are often left with only body memory.

It's not unusual for someone to forget most of what happened. I have almost no recollection of what occurred after the police arrived that evening. What I do remember are the scary bodily sensations I was left with in the first couple years that followed.

As they manifested, they caused me to question myself. You may ask similar questions:

Why do I shake?
Why do I curl up in a ball?
Why am I so anxious?

Why can't I stop the flashbacks from happening?
Why can't I concentrate?
Why can't I remember things?
Why do I dissociate?

One day my friend Mary, who was living with me at the time, took me to the grocery store. While she was shopping, I told her I wanted to go back outside and sit in the car. I wandered around the parking lot for fifteen minutes looking for the car and couldn't find it. I felt like I was losing my mind! Often, I couldn't focus or remember much of what people would tell me; it was a scary time. As a therapist, I knew these feelings were to be expected, but that didn't make things any easier. Just know that they will get better with time. Be kind and patient with yourself, especially in the early months. It is not uncommon to feel hyper-aroused or totally numb. You have been through a highly traumatic experience losing someone to a death by suicide.

A simple practice that may be helpful when you're feeling either of these sensations is to give yourself a hug. Place your right hand on your left shoulder and take your left hand and place it under your right armpit. You can also try crisscrossing your arms and placing them on your chest. Sit with this and breathe. Feel your body and allow it to receive the comfort it needs. Notice if this holding creates any physiological shift.

Why did this happen to me?

In the weeks and months following a suicide, when shock and numbness abate, it's normal to question everything you once believed about the predictability of life. Traumatic events can profoundly perturb one's taken-for-granted constructs, sometimes shaking the very foundations of one's assumptive world.

You may wonder why a good God would allow something so horrific to happen to you. You may become untrusting of others and the world around you. You may believe you can't trust your own judgments or decisions. You may believe you can no longer trust God. This is all part of what therapists call the "meaning-making," each person has to work through.

To move forward, you will need to interrogate your own implicit assumptions about life, God and the world around you that were challenged by the trauma, while slowly groping your way toward new sustaining frameworks of meaning. The way you view life and the world around you will be forever changed. *You* will be forever changed. Others may not understand. To move forward, you will have to construct a new normal for your life.

Why would he/she do this?

Suicide feels like the ultimate form of rejection, especially for a spouse. As I mentioned previously, Mike told me he could never leave me; he loved me too much. Yet he did leave. In my rational mind, I knew how sick he had become, but in my more vulnerable moments, I struggle with why he didn't get help sooner. Why hadn't he fought harder for himself and for us?

In my irrational mind, I blame myself for not doing enough, not doing the *right* thing, and not getting the right treatment for him. In the next section, we will look at two different models for understanding and treating suicide. I've included this because had I known about these models I would have used the information to get my husband a different type of help. It also would have given me a better understanding of what was happening to him and why.

Understanding the drivers of suicide and getting the right help are everything when we're trying to save lives. If you're reading this book and you've been touched in some way by suicide, God may use this in your life to one day help someone else before it's too late. Perhaps it will even help assuage some of the angst and confusion you're feeling now as a survivor.

Why did he/she leave me?

Following on the heels of rejection, suicide leaves us feeling abandoned and betrayed by our loved one. You may question your value and worth. You may be angry, feeling like you mattered so little that your loved one would do something so terrible to you. The stigma of being abandoned leaves survivors feeling discarded and devalued. It's like your loved one said, "You're not worth sticking around here for."

It's one thing to have a spouse die from a prolonged illness they didn't choose, but it's quite another to have them seemingly *choose* to take their life. I hope by the end of this book I can help you better understand that your loved one was sick, and that each person who takes their life believes they *had* to die; even if they were people of strong character and faith.

Your loved one *really* believed you would be better off without them. They were not thinking with a sound mind. Ninety percent of people who die by suicide have a diagnosable mental health disorder at the time of their death.[4] The suicide wasn't about you, nor was it your fault. I know it feels like it was, but I pray that in time, you will be able to see this truth more clearly.

Why couldn't I have stopped it?

Perhaps the most difficult of the why questions for me personally was: *why couldn't I have stopped it?* This creates an enormous sense of guilt, making the trauma more complex. Being a therapist only made it worse for me. After the *whys* came the *should haves*. I should have forced Mike to get help sooner. I should have come back with him that day on the airplane from our home in Florida. I should have been more reassuring on the phone the night before. I should have had him committed. I should have, I should have, I should have. In my mind, I was as guilty as if I had pulled the trigger for him.

As survivors, we have to come to terms with the fact that there was nothing we could have done to stop it. Or, as we'll see in a later

chapter, realizing we did the best we could under terrible circumstances. To heal, I had to come to a place where I could hold on to
the belief that Mike, and Mike alone, chose to pull the trigger that
night. My dreams to save him often reflect my helplessness, and I
find myself once again struggling to accept his decision.

I have had people in my suicide loss group, and people I've met
as I go around the country speaking, who didn't even realize their
loved one was in such despair. One person shared a recorded video
chat they had with their grown child. The conversation was pleasant,
filled with joking and laughter. Right after the call ended, he took
his life. This parent had no idea their child was considering suicide.

The immediate response to a tragedy of this magnitude is shock
and disbelief. It was so incomprehensible for any of us to think that
Mike Schulte would do something like this. We all believed he was
invincible. No one could understand. His dental office was a beacon of
light to so many. He prayed with patients, ministered unselfishly to the
community, did free dental work, started a ministry in Nicaragua, and
presided over a crisis pregnancy center for thirteen years. He always
encouraged others to never give up, because of his unwavering faith.

I can only remember one time in our history together where my
husband was depressed and anxious, and it only lasted a few months.
Mike was cautious and untrusting of others at times, but nothing
like the paranoia that he exhibited in the last few months before he
died. Afterwards, everyone was asking the why questions.

Perhaps you're asking why too. Perhaps you think in order to move
on you have to *know*. But healing won't be found in the knowing.
There is no life there. What we can know is this: our loved ones didn't
take their lives to hurt us; they took their lives to end the incomprehensible and very personal torment they were living in. In order to heal,
we must at some point surrender our right to know or understand all
the answers we so desperately seek.

If I'm honest with myself, my search for answers is really a search
to disprove my belief that Mike wanted to leave me. I already know

that is a lie. I know in my heart Mike didn't ever want to leave me because he told me so on many occasions. But none of that assuages the sadness that gnaws at my soul. There is really only one thing I need, someone to heal my shattered heart. Enter Jesus.

Real healing can be found, and I have found it, in the arms of a loving God, who promises to lift us out of the slimy pit and give us a firm place to stand (Ps. 40:2).

Of course, we need to ask the why questions, and others need to be patient with us as we do so because it's in the questioning that we try to make meaning. This may take a long time. It did for me. The truth is, only God knows the answers to all our whys, and one day, some of those answers may be revealed, or they may not.

Eventually, we must move to a place of *acceptance* and transition from "why?" to "what's next?" To do that, we have to begin that meaning-making process. This may seem like an impossible task for survivors because suicide is so incomprehensible to us. How can we begin to understand why our loved one would desire to die and leave us behind?

In the next chapter, I'll share what suicide researcher Thomas Joiner learned about suicide and the desire to die. Joiner brings the dual awareness of survivor (his father died by suicide) and scientist to the fields of psychology, neuroscience, and genetics. His model for understanding suicide helped me understand why someone would desire to die by suicide, as well as the tremendous sense of burdensomeness our loved ones felt.

Sit with this for a moment. I know it doesn't make sense to a rational mind, especially because we may feel such profound hurt, rejection, and anger at our loved one for leaving us, but our loved ones weren't operating with a sound mind that would have allowed them to make the swing back from being that clinically depressed to rational thinking. They most likely dissociated and thus were able to complete the suicidal act. I pray as we unpack this in the next chapter, it may help you heal in some small way and give you greater compassion for the enormity of pain your loved one was in.

If you're angry, it may help you forgive your loved one for leaving. I know many of you may be dealing with guilt, shame, and regret, but in the end, please know that it wasn't your fault.

Consider This

1. How do you feel about Anne-Grace Scheinin's quote, "Suicide doesn't end the pain, it only lays it on the broken shoulders of survivors"?

2. What why questions are you asking?

3. Which "I should have" statements do you say to yourself?

4. Do you blame yourself for your loved one's suicide? If so, in what way?

5. Do you have a safe person to walk alongside you and help you with meaning-making?

Chapter 2

Making Sense
of the Desire to Die

*"How long, LORD? Will you forget me forever? How long will you hide
your face from me? How long must I wrestle with my thoughts and day
after day have sorrow in my heart?"*
—PSALM 13:1–2

On July 15, 1974, a few weeks before her thirtieth birthday, Christine
Chubbuck was reporting on a story of a shooting at a local restaurant
when the reel jammed, prompting her to shrug nonchalantly, turn toward the camera and proclaim: "In keeping with Channel 40's policy
of bringing you the latest in blood and guts, and in living color, you
are going to see another first: attempted suicide." She then drew a
revolver from below the news desk, placed it behind her right ear, and
pulled the trigger.[1]

Was this an impulsive act? According to Thomas Joiner, a leading
suicidologist, the answer is no. Joiner believes that even though many
people who take their lives give no clues to loved ones that things
have gotten so bad, they have been contemplating the act, sometimes
for years.[2] While it can appear that the suicide came out of the blue,
that isn't always the case.

If we look at the Chubbuck case and flip the pages back on her
life, we see that she had attempted suicide before. She had struggled
with depression for years, and in 1970, she took an overdose of
drugs. Contributing to her depression was the death of her boyfriend

in a car accident. Chubbuck was being treated by a psychiatrist at the time of her death. A week before her suicide, she told Rob Smith, the night news editor, that she had bought a gun, and she often joked about killing herself on air. She also interviewed a deputy sheriff and asked him if someone was contemplating suicide, what would be the best way to conceal the gun. On the air that morning, eyewitnesses reported that Chubbuck's left hand was shaking uncontrollably right before her right hand reached for the gun.[3]

What seemed to most people as an "out of the blue" random act on national television, was actually something that had been brewing in this young woman's mind for quite a while. "To view the suicidal act as impulsive," says Joiner, "that people take their lives on a whim, is to misunderstand the death of the suicidal person."[4]

Mike had been thinking of suicide for a while. He mentioned it only once, but I had no idea just how serious he was until three months before he completed the act and became really sick. The only time I saw him depressed, it was situational and passed after a couple months. How does someone like *that* decide to take their life? Let's take a look at Joiner's theory on suicide to get a sense of what was going on internally for my husband, and thousands like him, and what would birth the desire to die.

THE THREE-FACTOR MODEL

Thomas Joiner has been studying suicide for decades. He is a graduate of Princeton University and received his PhD in clinical psychology from the University of Texas at Austin. He is currently the Robert O. Lawton distinguished professor in the department of psychology at Florida State University (FSU), Tallahassee. His theory, the Interpersonal–Psychological Theory of Suicide Risk, may help lend some understanding to survivors trying to make sense of a seemingly senseless act.

In addition to his long list of credentials and honors in this field of study, Joiner operates a research laboratory for the Study of Psychology and Neurobiology of Mood Disorders, Suicide and Related Conditions. He is also a survivor of suicide loss. His interpersonal psychological theory is a three-factor model that helps answer two of the questions that can plague survivors:

1. How was my loved one capable of enacting lethal self-injury?
2. Why would my loved one desire to die?

To answer the first question, Joiner asserts that a person must possess the ability to enact lethal self-injury. This appears on the diagram below as those who are capable of suicide, meaning serious attempt or death by suicide. He posits that this requires a character trait of *fearlessness.*

> The acquired ability to enact lethal self-injury is a necessary precursor to serious suicidality, especially to completed suicide. This acquired ability involves fearlessness about confronting pain, injury, and indeed death.[5]

There are plenty of psychological explanations for this and a great deal of research, but for our purposes, let's just say that fearlessness is a combination of nature and nurture. My husband definitely had this quality, and I believe was born with it. He was a huge risk-taker, always lived life on the edge, and always pushed the limits.

You may be thinking: *My loved one was a gentle and meek person. There is no way he/she possessed the quality of fearlessness or demonstrated any type of risky behavior.* That may be true, but the intensity of emotional pain your loved one felt, even if it wasn't visibly shown, must have been present for them to have believed death was the only option. It mostly likely gave them the courage it took to end their life.

In the model[6] below, Joiner's concept of fearlessness as an "acquired ability" would be included in the circle "Those who are capable of suicide."

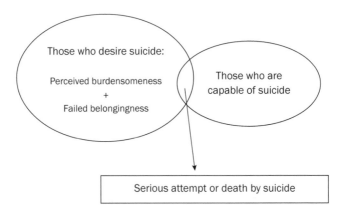

Used by permission from Harvard University Press

Let's be clear. Joiner *isn't* saying that a person isn't subject to fear. Remember, it was reported that Christine Chubbuck's hand was shaking violently right before she pulled the gun out. She was terrified.

As we'll see, sometimes that fear has saved people's lives. This happens many times when the brain's amygdala (fear center) kicks in and the suicidal person decides at the last second not to go through with the act. This happened to Mike on several occasions.

One night, I had come home from work late, and I thought he was in bed sleeping. I went into the sunroom downstairs to work on my computer. I hadn't been working very long when I heard gunshots going off in our back field. I ran screaming through the house calling Mike's name. No answer. It was like a tidal wave of terror hit me. I was shaking uncontrollably. I couldn't feel my own body.

Mike had been so depressed and anxious lately; had he actually tried to harm himself? I thought. I ran outside screaming his name over and over, only to see him moments later with a gun in his hand walking down from the field. Just then our son Michael drove up the driveway. I ran to Mike and collapsed on the driveway screaming and crying hysterically. Mike had made his first known attempt that night, but he couldn't go through with it. I'm thinking his amygdala kicked in just in time and thwarted the attempt, at least that one.

Kevin Hines is another person who experienced amygdala hijack. He jumped off the Golden Gate Bridge when he was nineteen years old. He said the second his feet left the rails, he knew he had made a terrible mistake—he wanted to live. But it was too late; there was no calling 911 for help in midair. Kevin was one of the few people who has survived this attempt. (You can hear his amazing story online.[7]) Kevin says he still struggles with depression, paranoia, and suicidal thoughts. He just knows what to do now when those toxic thoughts come.

To expound on this idea of fearlessness, Joiner posits that fearlessness can be something we are born with, or it can be developed through *habituation.* This means the more a person exposes themselves to risky behavior, the more they adapt to it until it no longer terrifies them. This is what Joiner references when discussing the acquired ability to commit suicide. Both concepts of fearlessness and a perceived sense of being a burden, as well as a thwarted sense of belonging, are a key component of the interpersonal psychological theory he developed.

Here is an example of how habituation works in an ordinary scenario. It's early May, and the pool in my backyard is now open and looks inviting. However, at the beginning of May in Virginia, I know the water will be cold. I don't want to jump in because I'm a wimp, but my little grandson Elijah is fearless. He jumps in and starts to squeal because it is cold, but what happens after he swims around for five or ten minutes? He gets used to the cold water. That's habituation.

Regarding the capability for suicide, Joiner drives home the point that "self-preservation is a powerful enough instinct that few can overcome it by force of will. The few who can have developed a fearlessness for pain, injury, and death, which . . . they acquire through a process of repeatedly experiencing painful and otherwise provocative events."[8]

This is *not* to say that everyone who can habituate to pain will commit suicide. They must also possess the two qualities pictured on the left side of the diagram, which address a different aspect of the question, "Why do people desire suicide in the first place?" Even if they possess the acquired ability to enact self-injury, why would they want to? The answer is a *perceived sense of burdensomeness* and *failed* (or thwarted) *sense of belonging*.

DESCENT INTO DARKNESS

You may be thinking that everyone experiences the emotions indicated on Joiner's diagram at some time in their lives: a thwarted sense of belonging and a perceived sense of burdensomeness, and you're right. That's not what *this* is. This kind of loneliness swallows you whole, drilling down on your soul so that you can't breathe. It's an inexplicable mixture of emptiness and terror that leads to a despairing of life.

How do I know? Because I witnessed it firsthand. I entered into it with Mike. I've touched the kind of darkness that people don't come back from. I experienced my strong, invincible husband slipping away from me like a terribly frightened child, and there was nothing I could do to save him.

I remember the last trip we took to Arizona with my son and his family. Mike's behavior had become more and more erratic. He and I went out to dinner alone one night. He thought the waiter and the people sitting near us had been planted by the FBI to watch him. He thought our phones were being bugged and our homes were being watched. He felt increasingly more fearful and paranoid. I think it was the article in the dental magazine he read that marked the beginning of the end. That's when I lost him for good.

Mike read about a dentist who had been under FBI investigation because he had overbilled his Medicaid patients. I recall the man owed the IRS a lot of money. After a two-year investigation, the FBI stormed into his office and seized everything he had. The man went to prison for several years.

I remember lying in bed with Mike one night and he told me how terrified he was that was going to happen to him. Mind you, all this was in his mind. He never did anything unethical in his dental practice. In fact, Mike regularly provided free care to those in need. He was a good man, but he was sick.

As I've thought about Joiner's theory, and I've tried to make sense of what happened to Mike, I can understand how such extreme depression, paranoia, and loneliness can isolate a person to the point that they feel they're a burden. Mike was used to being in control, yet he felt like a burden on me and voiced that on many occasions. Early one morning we were sitting up in bed, and he looked at me and said, "What's it like watching me fall apart?"

"It's horrible," I said, falling apart inside myself, but trying to appear strong for him.

Suicide is an agonizing response to unbearable loss. For those of us left behind, we are left to figure out what it was our loved one saw as so unredeemable that it could never be fixed.

My kids believe that Mike knew he wasn't going to get better and that he didn't want to live like he was living. All I remember are all the words spoken between us that told me he wanted to fight to live for me—for us. The descent into darkness was just too great for him. Although our loved one's pain was different, the pain we as survivors experience is comparable because it never really ends. Survivors of suicide loss face a lifetime of sorrow.

For the first few months, I could barely get out of bed. I was consumed with finding the answers to the whys. I wanted to die because I believed my actions, or lack of action had been the cause of Mike's death. There are no written words to explain the hell I was living in. I felt numb, dead, and unable to feel my own body at times. I remember how hard it was just getting in the shower. The only way I knew I was alive was feeling the pulsating water on my flesh. How does one live on, holding the belief that they are responsible for the death of the person they love the most in the world? I could see no reason to go on until . . .

I was staying at my daughter's house, and we were watching a movie with my granddaughters. It was the Disney movie *Brave*. I wasn't even paying attention, but when I looked up, I saw castles and heard Scottish accents. Mike and I had enjoyed an amazing trip to England and Scotland earlier that year. When I saw the castles on the screen something snapped. I tried to get up to leave the room and fainted in the hallway.

My daughter ran to my side and my son-in-law carried me up to the bedroom. All I remember is Ashley coming back into the bedroom and sitting next to me on the bed. With tears in her eyes (my daughter doesn't often cry), she looked into mine and said, "Mom, please try." That was it. I was determined to do just that. I had two children and five grandkids at the time; I had to move forward.

BELIEVING IN TRANSFORMATION

According to Joiner's model, a person holds these two psychological states simultaneously (fearlessness/burdensomeness). When they are strong enough and last long enough (sometimes years, sometimes months), a person can develop a desire to die. My husband experienced both those states for quite a while. He was convinced we'd all be better off without him. Mike was suffering from severe clinical depression, anxiety, and paranoia. A couple of days before he died, he told me he thought he was hearing voices. Perhaps your loved one showed these symptoms or, perhaps like those of Christine Chubbuck, the symptoms were hidden to you and most observers.

Whether they showed symptomatology or not, your loved one's struggle most surely didn't come out of the blue. Something was tearing at their soul; something they may have kept hidden even from you. Perhaps something that created shame and self-loathing. They may not have broken down in front of you. They may not have broken down in front of anyone, but I'm convinced all of them were dealing with some type of collateral damage—the things in life that had broken their hearts and shattered their souls in a way that made life unbearable. Each was carrying something that was too heavy for them to bear.

Even though our loved ones are gone, we can't allow this loss to destroy us and our families too. I know you may not even care about that right now. It may seem impossible to believe things will get better, that the pain will abate. Loss does that to us; it's like someone took a sledgehammer to your soul and you find yourself feeling more dead than alive.

My first book, *Shattered: Finding Hope and Healing through the Losses of Life*, was released two months before Mike took his life. People asked me if I thought God had me write the book to prepare me for this tragedy. I believe in some ways He did. Going back and reading some of my own words with regard to handling the losses of life is difficult, but actually *living out* those words would have been impossible without God's help. This passage reminds me of how I found my way out of unbearable darkness. I pray it for you as well.

If we're faithful to stay the course, transformation will flow from two sources: the *choices* we make about how we will handle our pain, and our *willingness* to be personally responsive to how God is leading us through this journey of brokenness.

Our first challenge, then, is to obtain a decided heart. That means that we must choose whether what's happened *to us* will be the most important part of our story, or whether it will be what happens *in us* in response to our loss.

If we choose the former, we will be tempted to define ourselves through the dark and cloudy lens that loss engenders. This can lead to self-pity, regret, bitterness—even addictive behavior— to hide the pain, thus hindering our growth and movement. But if we choose the latter, we will enlarge our capacity for God to work in our hearts, and we will be willing to accept the darkness in order to embrace the light—for both are intricately woven with loss. If we find the courage to choose this path, the most important part of the story will be yet to come.[9]

I don't desire to give you some neat formula to get through this. There isn't one. Nothing prepares you for something like *this*. Suicide is a different kind of loss, a different pain, and a different kind of suffering. Answers won't be the glue that holds the heart together for *this*. Each of us have choices to make about how this tragic event will impact our entire life trajectory. Those choices will do one of two things: propel us toward hope or lead us to despair.

It's been several years now since I lost Mike, and some days it still seems like I'm falling backwards. I'm tired of carrying the pain. I'm tired of missing him. I'm tired of all the milestones in my family's lives that he's not around to share with me. I'm tired of the things people still say to me. And I'm tired of being misunderstood. If you are too, keep reading. Together, we'll push through this darkness, and soon there will be a glimpse of light.

Consider This

1. Did Joiner's model help your understanding of what your loved one was possibly experiencing? Explain.
2. What conclusions have you drawn about yourself from this tragedy?
3. If you're experiencing guilt/shame, how is it affecting the way you're living? How is it affecting your connection to others?
4. Have you made any hope-filled choices thus far? How does that make you feel?
5. Can you envision what you want your life to look like in six months? A year? Describe.

The Silent Scream

*"I believe that the person who commits suicide puts his psychological
skeletons in the survivor's emotional closet—he sentences the survivor
to deal with many negative feelings and more, to become obsessed with
thoughts regarding their own actual, or possible role in having precipitated
the suicidal act or having failed to abort it."*

—Edwin Shneidman[1]

Looking back over the landscape of this wilderness journey, there were
too many days to count where I wondered if I would ever make my
way through the dense fog of despair. The immediate response was
shock. For me, this manifested as *derealization*. I not only couldn't
believe what was happening was real, but I also had the strangest
feeling *I* wasn't real. I felt as if I were outside out of my body, and my
mind couldn't ground itself to the present moment. It was frighten-
ing. If you've experienced this sensation, you understand.

Other feelings you may be experiencing include anxiety, difficulty concentrating, forgetfulness, trouble sleeping and eating, fatigue,
stomach upset, anger, sadness, hopelessness, and despair. All are normal responses to what you've been through. Don't let them frighten
you; in time, they will lessen. In a later chapter, you'll learn ways to
combat some of these distressful feelings.

You must realize that you have been traumatized by your loved
one's suicide. This is a loss unlike others. In her book *No Time to Say
Goodbye: Surviving the Suicide of a Loved One,* Carla Fine explains
the unique impact of this loss:

Coping with any death is traumatic; suicide compounds the anguish because we are forced to deal with two traumatic events at the same time. According to the *American Psychiatric Association's Diagnostic and Statistical Manual of Mental Disorders, the level of stress resulting from the suicide of a loved one is ranked a catastrophic—equivalent to that of a concentration camp experience.*[2] (emphasis mine)

As survivors, we try to move forward; however, the traumatized brain isn't always a willing participant, making even the most trivial tasks seem impossible. Just existing becomes an excruciating reminder of just how "abnormal" we feel. I remember sitting at my kitchen table with some dear friends one day, and they were all talking, laughing, and just doing life. I sat there thinking, *my husband has just killed himself and my life will never be the same!*

How can life go on with simple chatter or mundane tasks when your world has stopped, and you may feel as if you're dying inside? Eventually, as I did, you can find your way forward and into a new life; but in the immediate aftermath it is hard to see that as a possibility.

THREE AREAS OF IMPACT

I believe the damage and disruption of suicide leaves the survivor facing three areas of impact vulnerability. They are as follows:

The Traumatized Brain
Guilt and Shame
Crisis of Meaning

We will look at each of these areas separately in the hope that the knowledge you gain will help instill the hope that things won't always feel this bad. Because the traumatized brain isn't functioning properly, you may not only be experiencing scary bodily sensations;

your mind may also be filled with scary thoughts. As survivors, we are at greater suicidal risk ourselves because we are vulnerable to despair and feelings of hopelessness.[3]

Intrusive thoughts will come. I can remember driving in the car on several occasions and thinking how easy it would be to just crash into a tree or pull into a lane of oncoming traffic and end the pain. What can we do with such horrible thoughts? In a later chapter, we'll talk more about this, but for now realize it's normal to have them once reality sets in.

It's also normal to be hypervigilant about another loss occurring. I had parents in my suicide group who feared that a remaining child might be taken from them, leading them to constant overprotectiveness. Those who love the survivor are also struggling and no doubt fearful for their loved one. My own children were also very protective of me. The level of despair they saw in me over the first six months no doubt took a toll on them too.

I'm reminded of a former client I'll call Beth. She lost her son to suicide over a decade ago. Beth was a nurse in the ER, so she was no stranger to stress, trauma, or loss. She had always managed her emotions well in the past, but after her son's suicide, Beth noticed she couldn't regulate her emotions at all. She became increasingly hypervigilant about her other two children. If they didn't call, text, or contact her in any given situation, she would have a full-blown panic attack and be filled with terror.

Beth's responses to her son's suicide are often the norm for people who have been traumatized. They become terrified of experiencing another loss. The fear and terror they feel is directly related to what they felt the day their loved one died. That experience resides in the body and has to have a way out in order for optimum healing to occur.

In my work with traumatized clients like Beth, I knew I needed to first start working with her body. I taught her exercises to make her feel safe in her own skin again. She needed more than a cognitive processing of what happened to her son; that would come later. Her whole worldview about life was shattered and everything she thought was predictable and certain went up in smoke. This work took time, but it paid off. Beth found freedom and was able to write a new story that didn't include the debilitating fears she struggled with. She also had loads of support from the significant people in her life who loved and cared for her, which is a strong predictor of resiliency.

Thankfully, for me, with time, lots of help and several grandbabies, I no longer struggle with wanting to take my own life. I tell you this because I want you to believe that how you feel now will not be how you feel next year, or the year after, or the year after that. I'm not suggesting it will be easy, but you *will* get better. I've not only experienced it, but I've seen others who have gone through similar circumstances emerge healed and whole again.

WHIRLWIND

The traumatized brain plays tricks on us. We are left feeling disconnected and can experience those troubling feelings of derealization-depersonalization, the sense that we aren't real and we're observing ourselves from outside our bodies. We can also feel robotic, experiencing emotional numbness and just going through the motions of living when we feel dead. This was, and still is, something that happens to me on occasion. These are very disturbing but common feelings for those who have experienced a traumatic event.

I've spent a great deal of time in suicide support groups, both as a leader and a participant. Some people have shared that they felt as if they were watching their lives on a movie screen. Others reported nightmares and feelings of intense and crippling anxiety. One woman explained that she couldn't focus, couldn't concentrate, and became extremely forgetful. She would stay in bed for days, not having the energy to get up. She experienced constant hypervigilance. All these experiences are indicative of the traumatized brain.

Before the first year following Mike's suicide had ended, a dear friend flew up to stay with me for a few days. Gail used to work at Mike's dental office when she lived across the street from us but had eventually moved back to her hometown of Atlanta. When she came to visit, we took the train to New York for two days to spend time together. I was still unable to fly (more on that later). I was somewhat worried about the cab ride home from the station because I had taken a cab home from the airport on that fateful November 12. Mike had left the day before me from our home in Florida.

Just as the cab turned the corner to one of the main streets to my house, I could feel my body becoming highly activated. I tried hard to control it, but eventually the experience of being in the cab overwhelmed me. As we drove up my driveway, Gail could see my distress, and told me to go inside and she'd be right there. When she came in after paying the driver, she was horrified to find me huddled in the corner of the laundry room shaking. This behavior pattern had become encoded in my brain. We psychotherapists call it *procedural memory*.

I was right back in the trauma, remembering how the cab pulled into the driveway that afternoon and I saw the garage door open with Mike's car still there. He was supposed to have left to go to a mental health treatment center that morning in Dallas to get psychiatric help, and I was to meet him there a couple of days later and stay with him for as long as was necessary.

Flashbacks such as these are like waking night terrors. But why? How can they be so vivid and real and carry with them such powerful visceral experiences? A simple explanation of what's going on in your brain can help ease the anxiety that goes along with all these horrible feelings and sensations. When I'm working with individuals who have severe anxiety disorders or have experienced a trauma, I find that teaching them a little about brain neurobiology, the "biological mechanisms by which nervous systems mediate behavior,"[4] is helpful. I know it was for me, so let's take a look.

HOW TRAUMA AFFECTS THE BRAIN

Your limbic brain is a set of structures that lie on top of your brainstem. These structures regulate your emotions and play important roles in memory consolidation and emotional regulation. The *amygdala*, for example, is a small almond-shaped structure that, along with the *hippocampus*, is responsible for emotional memory. Its job is to warn us of impending danger. You know it as the "fight or flight" response. "While it takes around 300 milliseconds for you to become aware of a disturbing event, the amygdalae react to it within 20 milliseconds!"[5]

When the amygdala fires, it releases hormones like adrenaline and alerts your brain's *hypothalamus*. It then signals your pituitary gland, which transmits hormonal signals calling for an emergency response. Your adrenal glands respond by pumping out cortisol. This hormone is great in small doses (preparing us for danger); the problem is, when the traumatic experience is replayed via procedural memory through flashbacks, the alarm system doesn't want to turn off, keeping cortisol at high levels. This occurs because your brain still believes the danger is present. Remember, to your brain, memory and time have frozen, and it's like the event is happening over and over in the here and now. It's what happened to me that day with my friend Gail.

Your rational brain is your *prefrontal cortex*. It is constantly being hijacked by the fear center, your amygdala. When flashbacks occur, the prefrontal cortex goes offline, meaning you can't think or reason well, if at all. You can't talk yourself out of your body's reaction. The key is learning techniques to bring your prefrontal cortex back online. In short, your brain has been programed for reactivity by the traumatic event and your fight/flight/freeze response kicks in even when there isn't any impending danger.

I recall sitting in our sunroom one day with several visitors. Suddenly, my gaze landed on a hole in the cathedral ceiling—it was where the bullet exited our master bedroom, above. Needless to say, I went into a full-blown flashback, shaking, crying, and running to the stairway in an attempt to go upstairs to the bedroom to stop Mike. My brain was frozen in the past.

This state of constant hyperarousal keeps these chemicals releasing in your body, which over time, can cause stress-related health issues. That's why learning to calm yourself is so important.

Think back to those *why* questions. One of them was, *Why is this happening to me?* Why does the amygdala become so activated? Because subconsciously, it's processing information from the senses and our *past* experience: the traumatic event. It concludes danger without the input from the more logical prefrontal cortex. This ramps up the autonomic nervous system by elevating heart rate, respiration, blood oxygen levels, and blood flow to muscles in order to prime us for the fight or flight response. It also deactivates nonessential bodily systems. In other words, when you're terrified, remembering what you had for breakfast or what you were wearing isn't important. Those systems shut down in lieu of the presenting danger.

There's also another response: freeze/collapse. You see it in animals when they are being preyed upon; they play dead. My response to finding my husband was to flee, but then to collapse. You may be experiencing both, which is normal.

The *thalamus* is the part of the brain responsible for relaying sensory input to the cerebral cortex; along with the hippocampus it also plays a role in memory. This explains why a traumatic event isn't remembered as a coherent narrative with a beginning, middle, or end, but only as isolated sensory imprints, sights, and sounds. These can be accompanied by physical symptoms of terror and helplessness. A trauma survivor doesn't know how to tell the story because there is often no memory. We're trying to weave the splintered pieces of self into a rational narrative—and there isn't one for something like this.

Remember I said the body keeps score? For me, sensory imprints from the trauma left me curling up in a ball, or totally dissociating when I was triggered. I could go from total hysteria one minute to totally frozen the next. I couldn't speak when spoken to, and it was obvious to others that I wasn't present in my own body. It was as if I were in a daze, somewhere far away and out of touch with reality. I had trouble remembering things, and I wasn't able to sequence events with clarity.

To help bring my prefrontal cortex back online, my family and friends were shown how to help. They would get close to my face, talk softly but firmly, and have me make eye contact. They would assure me that everything was okay and that I was safe. There is something powerful in the meeting of the eyes, which would re-ground me to the present moment, especially with my daughter Ashley.

Finally, we come to the part of the brain that encodes memory: the *hippocampus*. Think of it as your brain's chronologist, responsible for retrieving and storing memory. Your hippocampus works in sync with your amygdala to encode each of your experiences into memory.

Remember, however, that when you've experienced a traumatic event, the amygdala keeps firing as if you're still in danger. Your hippocampus, on the other hand, shuts down. It makes sense if you think about it. Memory isn't important when you're facing something life-threatening, so your body prioritizes the signal from your amygdala and puts the signals from the hippocampus on the back burner.

Remember too that in response to stress, the body releases cortisol. When that stress becomes chronic, too much cortisol can actually damage cells in the hippocampus. In short, during a traumatic event, the hippocampus does not function properly, so it isn't doing its job storing memory. After the danger has passed, the only recollections one may have from the trauma are *somatic*, sensations stored and felt in the body. Later, if you encounter things that remind you of the event, your amygdala retrieves that memory and responds in the moment as if the danger is once again present in the here and now. Because the body keeps score, we have to allow it to speak. We have to learn to befriend all those scary sensations and feelings that go along with a traumatic event and learn that they won't destroy us.

SO WHAT?

Understanding what is happening in your brain may help assuage the fear that you're losing your mind; but you still may be thinking, *So what? Understanding isn't helping my symptoms.* You're right. Your symptoms won't be ameliorated by head knowledge alone, because as you've learned, parts of your brain shut down and leave you with only visceral knowledge.

While a lot has been learned about post-traumatic stress and trauma over the past decades, we still don't understand why people have different responses to trauma. The symptoms WWI soldiers experienced, including paralysis and amnesia, are not even listed in current editions of the *Diagnostic Statistical Manual of Mental Health Disorders* because that language is outdated, and new criteria have been set as markers for PTSD.

Why is it that some people can go through a traumatic experience and bounce back in time, while others stay stuck for years? We'll tackle some of those questions later, but what is clear is that the fallout from any traumatic event is real and carries with it lasting scars. Columbine survivor Sean Graves regularly finds himself back at the Columbine High School shooting, reliving the nightmare of that day that claimed the lives of thirteen people and wounded twenty others.

Graves, who was fifteen at the time, lost his closest friend in the shooting. He reports recurring nightmares of bullets firing into his stomach, back, and foot. His injuries ended his dreams of enlisting in the military or becoming a police officer. He says he worries about sending his three-year-old daughter to school, and every April, his mind replays the details of that fateful day when two classmates clad in trench coats opened fire on students and teachers. He says he finds himself back on the cold ground with fire alarms ringing and gunshots firing.[6]

Columbine's former principal Frank DeAngelis has spent the last twenty years reaching out to shepherd other communities and principals who have been victimized by random school shootings. He explained his residual response to the traumatic event:

> "It's funny what your mind does in a crisis situation . . . I don't remember hearing the blare of the fire alarms. I guess I blocked out the sound but I remember the strobe lights flashing. I also remember exactly how those shots and the glass shattering behind me sounded."

DeAngelis has also learned to avoid driving in springtime. He has crashed his car six times since the shooting, each time around the anniversary. Now he relies on Uber and Lyft rides for a few months.[7]

It's still fascinating to me how the body remembers dates and anniversaries. Graves said his nightmares are like clockwork beginning in April, even when he's unaware of the month. I too still struggle with dreams about Mike, only they aren't about the suicide anymore. If this is happening to you, it's because your subconscious is trying to make sense out of what happened. If your situation was complex, leaving you with unfinished business with your loved one, your dreams may be a way your subconscious is trying to finish the story.

Meaning-making about a traumatic event is an important topic we'll cover later, but for now, our purpose is to answer one question: *How do I start to feel better now?* The answer lies in calming down the traumatized brain. The first step is simple: you learn to *breathe*.

EXERCISES

Jar of Grief Exercise

The image below of three jars is one of my favorite ways to conceptualize the journey we are on as survivors of suicide loss. The corresponding exercise can be used with any loss. The visual helps me illustrate an important message for those I'm counseling: it doesn't matter if you're at year one, year ten, or year twenty, you will never forget your loved one. You will find a place to put your pain, but it will always be there, reminding you that this is a part of your story—not a part to be deleted because it was tragic, but a story of deep abiding love and redemption. For me, that included the love I shared with Mike, and the love I share with God. Once Mike was no longer my earthly husband, God stepped in to care for me and provided everything I needed.

The "ball in a jar" concept was developed by Barbara Monroe, who was expanding upon the work of the late Lois Tonkin, a grief counselor.[8] I will explain how it works—and how I use this exercise to help others—using the events of my experience as an example.

The small jar on the left represents my world at the beginning of my grief journey. At that time, the ball representing my grief just barely fits inside that small world. There is no space for me to breathe or move around my grief, or to think of anything else. I was totally immobilized in the early months. I barely got out of bed. I was riddled with fear. I couldn't sleep without medication, and I couldn't eat. I cried, or I was numb, staring into space. I couldn't think of anything but Mike.

After a while, I was ready to expand my world . . . *a little*. The grief (the ball) doesn't shrink; rather, my world (the jar) becomes larger. As I ventured out again, meeting new people and engaging in more activities, my world began to expand. As I continue to enlarge my world with more activity, the grief *stays the same*, but I'm able to more easily move around it.

So, I will keep enlarging my world. For me, that looked like going back to work; it could mean finding a new career, it could be making new friends, or finding a new place to live. All the while, however, the grief stays inside my heart and finds its own place in my world. What does this do? It honors my pain and my loved one forever.

Consider This

1. Do some journaling today. Write for at least five minutes. Record how you feel about Edwin Shneidman's quote at the beginning of the chapter. Just put your pen to paper and see what comes up.

2. What tricks is your brain playing on you?

3. Which response do you resonate with more: fight, flight, or freeze? Record any insights as to why.

4. Do you notice any symptoms of depersonalization or derealization? Do you ever feel robotic? Numb? Explain.

5. Have you thought of harming yourself in any way? If so, have the courage to share your feelings with a trusted therapist or family member. Seek professional help as soon as possible if these thoughts do not abate. That means if you can't function, if your sense of hopelessness lasts for more than two weeks, or if you start making a plan to take your life, call a suicide hotline immediately, see your doctor for an evaluation for possible medication, and see a therapist.

6. Are you having recurring dreams or nightmares? If so, is there a pattern or theme?

7. What steps can you take right now to bring some calm into your life? Examples might include listening to soothing music, taking a warm bubble bath, delegating some responsibilities to others, exercising, and/or praying.

Chapter 4

The Mind-Body Connection

"When things change inside you, things change around you."

There is a verse in the Bible that teaches that we are three dimensional beings with a body, soul, and spirit (1 Thess. 5:23). Because we have these three very different dimensions, it doesn't mean that these parts aren't intricately interconnected, each masterfully in sync with the other. This was no accident and was designed by God for the purpose of making humans unique. He breathed the breath of life into us. The breath is everything.

If you've lived long enough, the one thing you've most likely learned about life is its unpredictability. While we'd all like to think we can control the outcome of events, other people's choices, or tragedies, the truth is we only have control over *one* thing: ourselves.

When we face a traumatic event, it throws us off balance in each area, disrupting the equilibrium that allows us to feel in control of even the simplest thoughts and bodily sensations. Being unable to control the flashbacks, bodily responses, and the triggers surrounding the trauma can be terrifying, leaving us feeling unsafe, insecure, and profoundly vulnerable.

The most powerful tool you and I have to help regulate our emotional responses and allow us to regain some control in moments like this is our breath. Yep, you read that correctly. Research has proven that the best way to calm an overcharged nervous system is something we do every moment—breathe. Not just any kind of breathing, but slow, controlled, intentional breathing.

The American Institute of Stress explains the benefits of deep breathing:

> Abdominal breathing for 20 to 30 minutes each day will reduce anxiety and reduce stress. Deep breathing increases the supply of oxygen to your brain and stimulates the parasympathetic nervous system, which promotes a state of calmness. Breathing techniques help you feel connected to your body—it brings your awareness away from the worries in your head and quiets your mind.[2]

In the early stages of grief, you may only be able to practice breathing for a few moments. That's okay. For now, the most important part of mindful noticing is developing an awareness of your body and your breath. I believe noticing will be a key piece to your healing. Why? Because you can't change what you don't notice, and many times, when we're overcome by fear, stress, and anxiety, the first thing to go is our breathing. We may hold our breath, breathe too shallowly, or breathe too quickly.

JUST BREATHE

Since most traumatic memories are somatic, meaning these sensations are stored in the body, you need to anchor your awareness to your body first. As we move on, I'll teach you how to feel grounded and steady as well. To begin this practice, I'd like you to just spend the next few days paying attention to your breathing; especially when you sense your system becoming upset. Just notice, nothing more.

I know it will be difficult, but give it a try. Maybe record what you notice in a journal. So, begin here, noticing your breath. When you sense activation and a shift in your breathing, notice what triggered it. Notice what time of day it is, notice who you're with and what was being said. Notice how your internal monologue affects your breath. Is there a connection between your thoughts, what you're telling yourself, and how your body breathes?

After you've spent a few days paying attention, you can start learning how to breathe to engage the calming effects of your parasympathetic nervous system. Think of this as your body's brake system. Engaging this system will slow your heart rate, respiration, digestion, and blood pressure.

The practice will bring your body back to homeostasis, particularly if it's been activated. I'll explain different ways to do deep breathing, and you can choose which one fits best for you. To begin, find a comfortable, quiet place where you won't be distracted. You can do these exercises sitting in a comfortable chair or lying down.

Diaphragmatic Breathing

Diaphragmatic breathing is also known as "belly breathing," and it's done by contracting the diaphragm, a large muscle between the thoracic cavity and the abdominal wall. If you've ever watched a baby breathing when they're asleep, you may have noticed the rise and fall of the belly rather than the chest. That's the difference with this type of breathing. As you breathe in, your belly expands, not your chest. To check your own breathing technique, do this simple self-test.

1. Place one hand on your belly and one hand on your chest. Watch which hand rises first. If it's the hand on your chest, you're not "belly breathing." Can you breathe using your belly only so that your tummy moves up and down while your rib cage and upper hand do not move?

Now try this:

2. Lie on your back, place one hand on your chest and the other over your stomach.

3. Close your eyes. Take a breath in through your nose, and lift your stomach up about an inch with each inhalation you take.
4. Then relax to exhale through the nose, lowering your belly.

The idea is your belly (not your chest) should elevate during the inhale, and it should lower back down during the exhale. Repeat this exercise for three minutes.

Relaxation Breathing

1. Begin by sitting or lying down in a comfortable position. If you're sitting, make sure to uncross your arms and legs and sit with your back against your chair. Your eyes can be open or closed; I recommend closed.
2. Close your mouth and quietly inhale through your nose to the count of four.
3. Pause and hold your breath, then, exhale very slowly so that it takes a total of eight counts to return to the bottom of your breath. It's a long exhale and you should be straining to do it initially.
4. Pause.
5. Repeat for four full breaths and work your way up to eight breaths over time.

It's not uncommon to feel a little lightheaded, dizzy, or a dreamy-like state when you first start this practice. That's what we want. It's a sign you're engaging the parasympathetic system and your body is starting to calm.

BRINGING THE BODY BACK TO BALANCE

To begin the process of teaching my clients about noticing, and to help them understand the mind-body connection, I not only teach them breathing exercises but also teach them how to scan their bodies for stress and tension. The idea is to learn focused attention skills that will help them control the regulatory circuits of the brain and heighten awareness using the five senses. This will help them alter the explosive flow of energy in their bodies that can derail them at times of intense grief and hyperarousal.

Doing a body scan helps you notice where you hold tension in your body. This focused exercise will help train you (and your brain) to slow down and pay attention to what your physical body is experiencing throughout the day. We are wise to pay attention to what our bodies are trying to tell us. This exercise should be done at least twice daily for ten minutes each.

Body Scan

Before each body scan, allow yourself a few deep breaths before you begin to relax yourself. Find a comfortable place to sit. Close your eyes. Breathe in and exhale out slowly.

Now, start at the top of your head and simply focus your attention there. Take your time with this exercise. Does your head feel heavy or light? Notice your temple area. Do you feel any pressure there? Do you notice you tend to furrow your brows?

As you breathe in and out, notice the sensations in your face. Is the face soft? Try to relax the face. Now, notice your nose. Feel the air going in and out of your nostrils. Does it feel warm or cool? Pay attention to how it feels. Pause. Breathe. Next, notice your eyes. Do they feel tired? Sometimes when I'm tired my eyeballs actually ache in their sockets. Focus your attention on your eyes. Next move down to your jawline. Do you notice you're clenching? If so, try opening and closing your jaw a couple times to relax it.

Notice if your top teeth are touching your bottom ones in a relaxed or tense manner. Notice your tongue. Remember, it's a muscle too, and sometimes when we're stressed, we push it hard against the top of our mouth or our teeth. Relax your tongue.

Now focus on the back of your head. Is there tension in your neck? Just notice any sensations that you may be feeling. Is there tightness or stiffness? Observe those sensations. Maybe move your head to the right and then to the left toward your shoulders.

Be curious about the state of these sensations. What might they be trying to tell you about your body? Stay focused. If you find your mind starting to wander, that's okay; simply redirect it back to whatever you're observing.

Move down your neck to your shoulders. What do you feel? Does your body feel warm or cool? Stay open-minded throughout this exercise. Move down to your elbows and your forearms. Do you have your arms relaxed? Are your hands folded, or are they lying openly next to your body? What do you notice about your hands? Are they warm or cold? Observe those sensations. Are your fingers open or closed? Relaxed or tensed? Keep focusing.

Now move to your chest. Notice your breathing here again. Focus on the rise and fall of your chest in conjunction with the breath. Are you breathing slowly? Are you holding your breath? Do you notice your breathing has relaxed you or not? Feel your chest going up and down. Focus all your attention there for a few moments.

Now move to your stomach. Oftentimes when we are stressed, we'll feel like we have a knot in our stomachs. Strong emotions can make us literally feel nauseated or tense in the gut. Observe any sensations you're holding in your belly and make a mental note of why they might be there. No judgments, just noticing.

Next, focus on your spine as you're seated in the chair. Do you feel anything there? Imagine your vertebrae holding up your spinal cord. Focus on any sensations in your back. Does it feel relaxed or tense? Now move to your legs. Focus on how they feel planted firmly on the floor. Move from your thighs down your calves. Do this slowly. What do you notice? Pause. Breathe.

Now focus on your feet. If you're wearing shoes, try wiggling your toes inside your socks. Feel the texture of your socks on your skin. Feel and focus on your feet inside your shoes. Move your feet around a little to feel them grounded on the floor. Notice how they feel. Sore? Tired? No sensation? Finish with a few deep breaths.

Notice if your state is more relaxed now. Make a mental note of which parts of your body are holding the most stress and tightness. Which parts are relaxed? Now, open your eyes. What do you feel? Has there been a shift in your overall state? Does your body feel more relaxed? If so, how? What made the most difference? Record your insights.

The body scan is a great way to improve your awareness. Is it easy to stay focused, or is it hard? Does your mind constantly wander? Or is it easy to stay on track? What things distract you? Are you sidetracked by your thoughts, emotions, or memories? It's okay if you notice you're continually distracted. That doesn't mean you're doing anything wrong. You're just observing your patterns, taking note of how often your mind is tempted to wander.

The point of breathing and body scan exercises is to teach you a deeper awareness of your body and help you learn to be a regulator of your own autonomic nervous system. It's like working out; the more you lift weights, the stronger your muscles become and the easier it is to do. The more you practice breathing, the calmer you will become.

Distress Tolerance

Grief is hard on the body, activating every system. The next exercises will help you learn to self-soothe. This concept has its roots in attachment theory and begins at the time we're born. In a nutshell, attachment theory is a theory of relationships, the closest kind of relationships. In infancy, it begins with the mother-child bond. The infant will instinctively form an attachment bond to the primary caregiver who is emotionally attuned and available to them.

The heart of attachment is proximity seeking behavior, meaning the child looks for and moves close to the caregiver when stressed or fearful. Why? Because closeness calms the system. In infancy, the baby is using the mother's system to regulate and calm its own. Therefore, the mother becomes a secure base and safe haven for the child. Babies are soothed through the sucking response, a calming voice, direct eye contact, and physical touch from the mother.

Physical touch is a beautiful way to feel the safety, security, and calming presence of another. So, touch can be a regulator, but it can also be an activator of the autonomic nervous system, depending on a person's past experiences. If you never learned that relationships were safe and secure, or if you've had any abuse in your background, before you try any of these exercises, make sure your body is okay with physical touch. Always honor what your body needs.

EXERCISES

These self-soothing exercises will help to calm your nervous system and ground you to the present moment. Here are a few to try with a trusted friend or partner.

Exercise 1

Before you begin this exercise, you can put a favorite essential oil on your hands. Take a moment to breathe it in.

1. Ask someone you feel safe with to sit next to you.
2. Have that person place their hand on your arm or your back.
3. Breathe gently in and out. Feel the sense of safety and warmth that this individual brings.
4. With your safe person still present, run your hands back and forth over the top of your legs and notice the texture of your pants. Then, bring your hand to your face and breathe in the scent of the essential oil. Stay here for as long as necessary.

Exercise 2

1. If you have an essential oil or a scent you love, put some on your hands before you begin this exercise. Then, find a comfortable position to sit and bring your hands to your face, breathing in the scent. Take a couple long deep breaths in through the nose and out through the nose.
2. Visualize a moment when you felt safe and secure. It could be with someone you love, or you could imagine being in some place you love. The point is, this recollection makes you feel secure and safe. Focus on this feeling or person of safety.
3. As you think of this moment of feeling safe, let yourself go with that. Breathe it in. Let the sensations of this experience engulf you. Stay with these feelings for as long as you are able. The longer you can hold the pleasant sensations, the stronger that feeling will become in your neural circuitry.
4. Repeat this practice several times a day.[3]

Exercise 3 Pendulation: Toggling Between Tension and Ease

1. Identify a place in your body where you might be holding a bodily sensation of a traumatic moment, or just something that feels unpleasant. Notice the physical sensations.

2. Now locate a place in your body that is not feeling any distress or trauma—maybe your elbow. Focus attention on that calm, untraumatized place in the body, steadily feeling the sensations there of ease and relaxation.

3. Now intentionally toggle your attention back and forth between the pleasant physical sensations of the place in the body that is not traumatized and the unpleasant physical sensations of the place in the body that is holding the network of the traumatic memory.

4. Repeat the toggling between the unpleasant and pleasant sensations for several rounds, gradually increasing the amount of time you spend focusing on the pleasant experience. Notice if the unpleasant sensation shifts or fades.

5. When the intensity of the unpleasant seems to have faded a bit, pause and reflect on the entire experience, noticing any shifts.[4]

Silence and Solitude

It may be helpful for you to journal about how these exercises feel for you. When the torrents of grief overwhelm you, turn to these to help bring your system back into balance. They may not help every time, but with continued practice, you should begin to notice some changes. After you complete your breathing and soothing exercises, I encourage you to sit with God and pray.

You may be thinking, *Silence and solitude is the* last *thing I need right now!* The very mention of it can evoke anxiety. Here's the thing, you won't be alone. God will be with you. That's the only motivation I had to go there. I needed something that even those dear folks who were walking alongside me couldn't provide—I needed the transforming presence of a God who loves me and promises never to leave me.

I needed to find God in the midst of this nightmare, and as I'd done so many times before in my life when tragedy hit, I went searching for Him with all my heart. Sometimes that looked like wailing uncontrollably, poring through my Bible until I received a word that comforted me; and in that dark night of the soul, God always showed up and did just that.

Sometimes, I felt guilty about my out-of-control emotional state, and I would try to hide my tears because I wanted to be strong. On many occasions, I would slip quietly up to my daughter's bedroom and cry alone. Perhaps your mind is struggling to keep a tight rein on your emotions too. Once again, I remembered a line I wrote from *Shattered:* "Our tears are the heart's attempt at healing, watering the dry and arid places of our soul, bringing us back to life and feeling. Your feelings are trying to expose your pain; do not do them the injustice of denial."[5]

Wherever you are in this journey, be authentic with yourself, with others, and with God. I believe the most important part of our grief work is found in these moments of silence and solitude, alone with Him, because that's when His heart touches ours. That's where He helps us uncover our greatest fears and assures us that even though it feels like we're being asked to walk through what we believe is the impossible, He is always near and we're never alone.

Consider This

1. As you did your breathing exercises, did you find your mind wandering? If so, record what thoughts you had. Have these thoughts become set-in-stone beliefs? Explain.

2. What things in your life do you find yourself trying to control? What effect is it having on your soul?

3. What part(s) of your body do you notice holds the most stress?

4. What activities that rest and restore your body can you use to reduce stress?

5. How does physical touch by another person feel for you? Is it comforting? If not, record your thoughts.

6. Do you find silence and solitude difficult? If so, why?

7. What fears are you dealing with? Can you trust God with them? Why or why not?

8. In what ways has God shown His care for you through this time of suffering?

9. What replenishes you spiritually? Spend time there caring for your spirit.

Chapter 5

Making Meaning

"Grief actually kills two people, the first one dies and the second one doesn't really want to go on living, but somehow does."

–Love Beyond Stars[1]

Debbie came to see me because she lost her husband to suicide. It had been seven years and she still had not made much progress moving forward. She was stuck in the past, unable to look to the future because of her constant yearning for her deceased husband. Her intense preoccupation with his death wouldn't allow her to see a future without him in it.

Debbie, like many people who suffer from what therapists call "complicated grief," went through the typical stages of grief (denial, anger, bargaining, depression, acceptance) but never brought them to *resolution*. Her everyday habits like looking at his picture, talking to him, sitting in their "special room" with all his things didn't allow her to carry out the normal routines of life. She was unable to enjoy a life without him in it, which caused her to withdraw from any social activities.

Complicated grief doesn't get better over time; it actually gets worse. It is characterized by a deep sense of hopelessness and a lack of meaning and purpose. That's why my work with Debbie centered around helping her carve out an identity of her own. She had spent most of her life being emotionally dependent on her beloved husband, so she never discovered who she really was.

This can leave many folks like Debbie stuck for years, unable to move on. I explained to Debbie that change doesn't always happen with the big things in our lives after we face loss, but in the everyday habits and decisions we make moment by moment. It's normal to yearn for and miss our loved one, but these longings dissipate as the griever works through their feelings and integrates the loss into their life processes, what counselors call schema.

According to one researcher, "Although grief after suicide has much in common with other forms of complicated bereavement, especially traumatic grief, it differs in the unique reactions specific to it, among them shame, self-recrimination and *a personal search for meaning*"[2] (italics mine).

To do this work of meaning-making means the griever must come to terms with the loss through meanings that help to reorganize and expand their understandings of self, God, and the world around them. This is more difficult when the death is a suicide because of the abruptness of the death, the violence of the death, the accompanying mental health conditions that can be present for the survivor (PTSD), as well as the extraneous stressors that a death by suicide engenders.

In his book *Grieving a Suicide: A Loved One's Search for Comfort, Answers, and Hope*, Albert Y. Hsu explains how the complicated grief survivors of suicide loss experience is similar to that of combat vets:

> We have experienced a trauma on par psychologically with the experience of soldiers in combat. In the aftermath, we simply don't know if we can endure the pain and anguish. Because death has struck so close to home, life itself seems uncertain. We don't know if we can go on from day to day. We wonder if we will be consumed by the same despair that claimed our loved one. At the very least, we know that our life will never be the same. If we go on living, we will do so as people who see the world very differently.[3]

Because survivors will see the world differently after the initial shock and numbness wear off, it's common for them to feel depressed, guilty, or full of shame about their loved one's suicide. As a clinician, I believe the most important part of our work as survivors is to unpack the *meaning* we've attached to the suicide.

When I'm working with a client, that's where I start because that's where they're living their lives from. I want to know what they're believing about self, God, and the world around them *now*, because everything that they thought they had figured out about life, God, and other people isn't going to work after the suicide because a bomb's gone off in their lives, and everything they believe has come into question. So, they're going to be struggling with their belief systems.

What do they need? To experience a different reality apart from the despair they're living in. How does that happen? By helping them develop a willingness to *risk*.

You see, as survivors, we need more than an intellectual knowing that life can be different, or better, we need an *experiential* knowing of that. Why? Because what do we know neurobiologically about new experiences? They create new thought patterns. They bring new perspectives. They rewire neuro-networks (i.e., create new brain pathways). In short, they foster what therapists call post-traumatic growth.

The reality you are living in at the beginning of this journey is only a small way of looking at reality. It's hard to see that now, but you are capable of experiencing a different reality. This just takes time and will look different for each of us. For me, in the early stages of grief, simply seeing my kids and grandkids was a lifeline. None of those realizations would have happened if I hadn't had people in my life encouraging me to step out and take some risks.

What might taking risks look like for us as survivors?

Risk going to a grief or suicide support group
Risk making new connections
Risk going to church
Risk taking a trip
Risk doing things you used to love
Risk smiling or laughing

Risk dating (if your loss was a spouse)
Risk going back to work or volunteering somewhere
Risk doing things alone
Risk moving
Risk having another child
Risk getting remarried

CHANGING OUR FILTERING SYSTEM

So, where do we begin? How do we start this meaning-making process? I'll give you three Ts to help you remember what's necessary. The first is *talk*. You need to tell your story to someone. I had people listening to me for days, weeks, months, and even years, and several trusted friends still listen to me in moments when I struggle to make sense of this tragedy. We need safe people to do that with.

The second T is *time*. We have to understand that we are capable of growth in the context of suffering; it just takes *time* before *transition*—the third T—can occur. As we move through this traumatic experience, there is always this juxtaposition between strength and distress that we're trying to balance. It's not *either/or* (strength *or* distress); it's *both/and* (strength *and* distress).

Let me explain. Most of us tend to look at life in two ways: things are good or things are horrible. Consider that God has designed us to hold both, the pleasant and the unpleasant, the good as well as the bad, simultaneously.

On most occasions, when I would go into my therapist's office, I would be a hot mess. If I wasn't dealing with the guilt, I was struggling with recurring nightmares, feeling swallowed alive with grief, or dodging bullets from everyone who wanted to tell me how to live my life. As I would relate all this to her, she would start by having me slow down and take a few deep breaths.

Then she would ask me to look around her office and name three things I found *pleasant*. *Seriously, she has to be kidding me*, I thought.

I was so hyper-aroused I felt like I was going to explode, and she's talking to me about finding something pleasant in her office! That was the last thing I felt like doing, but I knew she was a good therapist, so I complied and shared my three items.

Then she asked me to describe to her the one item I found the most pleasant out of the three. As I was doing that, I noticed something. A gentle shift had occurred as I was describing the object or image I was focusing on. (I used the image of my grandbabies a lot when I couldn't choose an object in her office.)

I grew calmer. I became more grounded. Life didn't seem *so* horrible. Why? Because as I was focusing on my grandkids, I felt happy thinking about them. The image of their little faces brought joy to my soul. I found meaning and purpose in life because of them. I wasn't spinning cartwheels of joy, but I wasn't in a black hole either.

This has been a transformative exercise for me. I teach it to all my clients, and every single time they are describing something pleasant to me, I see a little smile come over their faces. When I point it out, they are surprised, but they have learned an invaluable truth that we all need to embrace—even in the midst of profound suffering, we can still find good. The bottom line is this: we can be moving toward growth, while still being in the struggle, and after this work is complete, transformation will occur.

Like the breathing exercises, these focusing exercises were helpful, but nothing was more beneficial for me than listening to the voice of God and spending time with Him. I pondered two powerful Bible verses day and night. Perhaps they will comfort you too.

> "But he knows the way that I take;
>   when he has tested me, I will come forth as gold." (Job 23:10)

> I will take refuge in the shadow of your wings
>   until the disaster has passed. (Psalm 57:1)

THE STORIES WE TELL

Who doesn't love a good story? They can be full of excitement, drama, fun, adventure, and sometimes even sorrow tugging at our heartstrings. A good story sits with you, makes you curious, and causes you to ponder the characters' lives in light of your own. That's why we resonate with story.

But what happens when we come to despise the story we're living? What happens when not only do we not get a happy ending, but we are left to endure a catastrophic one? You and I are telling life-altering stories, ones we didn't choose. Lots of emotions go along with that—it's normal and it's okay. But how we *live* out our stories, that's what's going to matter, and that's what's going to determine the legacy we leave behind.

Just like we enjoy dissecting a favorite movie that's had an impact on us, so we must take an introspective look into our own story to make sense of it in order to live it out in a way that will bring honor to ourselves. This dissection takes time and can be terribly painful, but we need not be afraid of it because we heal within the pain.

If you've ever had a deep cut, you know what I'm talking about. The wound is painful and it bleeds. But in time you see the gentle process of healing unfold—raw wound, to scab, and finally to scar. The scar reminds us of the story we've left behind, but over time (sometimes years) the scar fades and what's left is almost undiscernible, except to us. This doesn't for a moment suggest that what caused the wound wasn't part of our story, but a healing has taken shape and redefines what has happened to us.

And so it is with the story of your loved one's suicide. When the wound is inflicted, it seems as if the bleeding will never stop. Then one day, you notice a scab has formed. Perhaps a week later the scab gets torn off and the wound bleeds yet again. This process continues for what seems like an eternity, until one day you notice the scab has been replaced with a scar. It's there to remind you of the journey, of the courage it took to keep living when everything inside you wanted to die.

You will heal. You will go on. You will have terrible days when you feel like the life is being choked out of your soul. But you will also find that one day, you laugh. One day, you find something to be happy about, and you keep repeating those kinds of moments over and over until you find meaning and purpose again. When someone asks about the scar, you'll have a story to tell. And in the telling, you'll give them hope.

Stephen Joseph is professor at the University of Nottingham, of the Center for Trauma, Resilience and Growth. He says this about story:

> Human beings are storytellers. It is human nature to make meaning of our lives by organizing what happens to us into stories. *We live our stories as if they were true.* We tell stories to understand what happens to us and to provide us with a framework to shape our new experiences. We are immersed in our stories.[4] (emphasis added)

"We live our stories as if they were true." Stop for a moment and breathe that in. If our story is everything, then we have to examine if what we're believing about the details in the story are true. We have to examine the characters in our story, and we have to examine ourselves to make sure we're getting it all right. If we're not, if we're believing lies about ourselves or the other characters in the story, the consequences will impact our entire life trajectory.

BELIEFS, THE MOST POWERFUL THINGS WE CHOOSE

Anke Ehlers and David Clark reported that the engagement of negative, "catastrophic" thinking in the aftermath of experiencing traumatic events contributes to the development and severity of PTSD and people's lack of responsiveness to treatment. Such "negative" ideation has a self-sustaining forward influence.[5]

This simply means that holding negative thoughts about the traumatic event, telling ourselves a *negative, self-defeating story* and ruminating about it can contribute to the severity of PTSD. It can also perpetuate the idea that we can provide for our own needs without any help from others. Living in that kind of story makes us resistant to seeking help and will impact any forward movement.

The story you're telling yourself about your loved one's suicide is filled with lots of thoughts and beliefs, some of which may be *lies*. If you want to move toward healing, you have to unpack the meaning you've attached to your loved one's death, especially if you're holding blame. You also have to tell your story to make meaning out of what's happened to *you*.

The main characters in my story were obviously Mike and I, but there were our children, our grandchildren, his family, friends, and others who entered the story later. I had to take a hard look at the set-in-stone beliefs about Mike's suicide that I was holding. Was it indeed my fault that he took his life, or was it possible I was believing some lies? What were others believing, and how did that affect my soul? I had to make meaning out of it all, and I had to tell the story that only I, the closest person to Mike, knew.

I had to own what was mine to own, including any decisions I made that I regretted. Then I had to forgive myself, and then do the same with Mike. Even though there were so many loose ends, I had to make sense of the rest and build a coherent narrative around that. Here are a few beliefs I had to unpack:

It was my fault.
I should have. . .
I shouldn't have . . .
I'm responsible for Mike's death.
I'm a horrible person.

At the end of the day, we as survivors are already drowning in infinite regrets, so add that to any toxic beliefs we're holding, and you create more and more layers to the grief process. Looking back at my beliefs, no wonder I was in a black hole. If you haven't already done so, take a moment to think about this and do what I did above; make a list of any negative beliefs you may be holding about yourself or any other characters in your story. Set it aside for now; we'll use it later.

If carrying all that isn't not bad enough, there's the condemning silence survivors often face and the perceived judgment survivors feel from loved ones who retreat into their own pain and you don't hear from them anymore . . . from friends who must go on with their own lives, which leaves you feeling lost and abandoned. Perhaps you've felt that some people blame you in part for your loved one's suicide, so even a casual remark or opinion can trigger an avalanche of emotions on an already guilt-ridden psyche.

The belief systems we hold don't just appear overnight. We don't wake up one morning and simply decide we're unlovable, inadequate, or guilty. Our beliefs are birthed from the stories we've told ourselves since childhood . . . things that have happened to us from a young age that gave us messages about *who we are*. We get those messages in our first few years of life from our primary attachment figures—Mom and Dad.

For some of us, the messages we received from our primary caregivers were positive. For others, they were negative. For still others, those messages tore at the soul. The meaning we attach to all this leads us to develop the belief systems we hold about ourselves, God, and others.

As we grow up, our world broadens, and we get messages from other people about who we are. These messages either confirm or deny our already established beliefs about our value and worth. When children come into the world, they're asking questions. Those questions get answered through the thousands of daily interactions they have with their primary caregivers in the first few years of life.

Here are a few important ones:

> Am I loved?
> Am I valued?
> Will others be there if I need them?
> Are others emotionally responsive, attuned, and available to me?
> Is the world a safe place?
> Are others trustworthy?

If the answers to those questions are generally positive, kids grow strong hearts and form secure attachments. If those answers are negative, meaning their caregivers weren't emotionally attuned and available for them, children learn behavioral strategies to manage and cope in a world where they feel unsupported and unsafe. Children develop several responses to not feeling safe and secure:

1. Anger
2. Fear
3. Anxiety

These emotions help drive our behavioral responses. They become the filters through which we learn how to love and be loved. I was always anxious as a child, even though I came from a very loving family. There was a history of anxiety disorders in my family of origin and lucky me, I inherited those genetic predispositions. I always struggled with fear and worry. I couldn't bear when others were upset with me. To deal with that, I developed a coping strategy of being a people pleaser and a conflict avoider.

I was also a rescuer and fixer most of my life. I believed it was my job to help others who were in distress, but when Mike got sick, I was way out of my league. The truth is, I wasn't a trauma specialist; I knew very little about suicidal behavior. I believed that because I was a therapist, I should have been able to prevent Mike from taking his life. As you can see, my beliefs about fixing and helping others took root in my life long before I ever became a counselor.

Because one of the complicating factors of suicide bereavement is the burden of finding reasons to explain the death and the suffering from feelings of shame for not being able to prevent the death, blame is often turned inward to the survivor. When I wasn't able to save Mike, the enemy of my soul convinced me that I caused his death because of my flaws. I believed I was a horrible person, and all I wanted to do was die.

The truth is, there were things I should have done differently, and that's what I have to carry for the rest of my life. I should have come back with him on the plane from Florida that day. I shouldn't have trusted him to get to the treatment center in Dallas alone. Maybe you're carrying similar feelings of guilt. If so, I understand.

It took me a lot of years to work through all this and grant myself compassion and forgiveness. God also did some pretty miraculous stuff along my healing journey. But here's the key: no matter what you *did*, what you *didn't do*, what you knew, or didn't know, it's still not your fault. You know why? Because you're *human*—and being human means being subject to limitations. That's why we need God's help.

Why is all this important? you may be thinking. Because how you go about the meaning-making process of your loved one's suicide may be directly related to already established beliefs you hold about yourself, God, and other people. I believe that as you try to make sense of or construct a narrative around the suicide, you have to expose and explore your beliefs. And you have to, in time, be able to do it with empathy—for yourself and your loved one.

That even includes how you have learned to express grief and deal with loss. While loss and pain are inevitable occurrences in our lives, there is nothing we are less prepared to handle or discuss. They are uncomfortable topics and therefore easily avoided.

REMEMBERED RESOURCE PERSON

After the suicide, I spent over a year doing a therapy called Eye Movement Desensitization and Reprocessing (EMDR). In the late 1980s, Francine Shapiro, an American psychologist, developed EMDR as a breakthrough therapy with special capacity to overcome the often-devastating effects of psychological trauma.

During an EMDR session, the therapist helps the client focus on related negative thoughts and feelings that are still being experienced as a result of a traumatic event. The therapist helps the client decide which of these beliefs are still relevant and which they'd like to replace with positive thoughts and beliefs.[6]

I was doing a session with my counselor one day, and we were dealing with my beliefs and guilt surrounding Mike's suicide. She asked me to talk to Mike about it. She wanted to know what Mike would say to me about having caused his suicide. What is it that he would want me to know?

While I was hooked up to the bilateral brain stimulation machine, I began the process. What occurred for me in that session was a miracle. I saw myself sitting on the edge of our bed and Mike was standing over me holding my face in his hands. He was looking right into my eyes, and with all the love and tenderness I have ever felt, he said, "Rita, it's not your fault." Immediately the thoughts and beliefs became replaced in my brain with this image, and I have never looked back. The traumatic memories are replaced with this and several other powerful images I believe God gave me. This was a powerful turning point in my healing.[7]

I don't practice EMDR with my clients. What I use instead is a Remembered Resource Person (RRP).[8] Take a moment to imagine yourself going through the exercise:

First, you would choose an RRP. This is a person who knows (or knew) you intimately—someone safe. It could be a parent, a spouse, a friend, or your deceased loved one.

Once you have a person in mind, engage in a mini conversation. Ask that person to speak truth into your life. Because you both know each other so well, you will feel a strong sense of what that person would want to tell you.

This Remembered Resource Person is always available to you, so anytime you are in distress remember to use this exercise.

I encourage you to also try prayer. Bring any guilt or shame you're carrying to God.

WOUNDED PARTS NEED A VOICE

If you're experiencing guilt or shame from the suicide, you will undoubtedly experience a number of other feelings. See which ones below apply to you:

Depression
Anxiety
Fear
Isolation
Self-blame
Loneliness

These wounded parts need a voice; don't try to silence them. Talk about these feelings to a therapist or close family member or friend. If you bury them, you bury them alive. Sticking your head in the sand is a strategy that rarely works. Find a way to put words to what you're thinking, feeling, and believing because those beliefs are driving your behavior.

Remember, your actions will *always* follow your beliefs. My beliefs about Mike's death caused me to behave in the following ways:

I was immobilized.

I wasn't able to get out of bed.

I was having constant panic attacks.

I wasn't able to drive.

I wasn't able to eat.

I wasn't able to sleep.

I wasn't able to be present for my kids.

I wasn't able to talk about anything but the suicide.

I didn't want to travel.

I didn't want to be alone.

Look at the list where you wrote down your beliefs surrounding your loved one's suicide and record how those beliefs are affecting your behavior. Write that down in your journal.

GUILT AND SHAME

What is shame, and how does it differ from guilt? Guilt says I *did* something bad (behavior), and shame says I *am* bad (intrinsically). I believed that I was intrinsically a horrible person, undeserving of forgiveness because my mistake cost someone's life—the someone I loved most in the world. What I have come to believe about myself now is that while I did some things I will always regret, I am not a horrible person.

According to an article in *Positive Psychology*, a 2016 study that observed people's reactions to feelings of guilt, shame, and anger discovered this:

> People who felt shame were more likely to avoid eye contact than people who felt guilty. They also found that people who felt guilt were more likely to want to repair the damage they may have caused than people who felt shame. Those and other findings led

the researchers to conclude that: *"shame is characterized by the desire to hide and escape, guilt by the desire to repair."*[9]

This is where things can get dangerous for survivors of suicide loss. Shame grows through hiding, escaping, and keeping things secret. Hiding because of the stigma you feel will worsen the symptoms of PTSD. If you don't reach out to others for support, you won't get the empathy you need, and empathy is an antidote to shame. Shame can swallow you whole, but guilt is treatable (through the power of processing, forgiveness, self-compassion, and empathy). If you are holding regrets like I was, try asking yourself if it's possible to press into the guilt for whatever you regret, and let go of the shame.

If there has been a death/suicide, survivors have no chance to make the repair, so it's easy to slip into shame, especially if you were left with unfinished business concerning your loved one. Although you can't repair things with your loved one, you can repair your relationship with yourself. You can own what you feel you did or didn't do and forgive yourself for it in time. Suicide loss survivors don't get a do-over, and even if we did, there is no guarantee things would have turned out any differently.

The story below is an illustration of this. It came from one of the first booklets I read by the American Association of Suicidology. The story is titled "'If I only had . . .' A true tale of two mothers." You'll notice in my summary that both the mothers in the story did very different things with their daughters who were suicidal, yet neither had a chance to make any kind of repair in the aftermath. See what the story brings up for you:

There were two young women who died by suicide, both were around the same age and both had struggled with depression for many years. They refused professional help and stopped taking their meds when things seemed to be getting a little better.

Fearing for her daughter's life, one mother had her committed against her wishes for psychiatric care. She asphyxiated herself with her bedsheets.

The second girl's mother constantly urged her daughter to get help but refused to force her into any institution for psychiatric care, fearing it would only worsen her daughter's depression. One day, she took her life with an overdose of pills. Afterward, both mothers blamed themselves for their children's suicides. The irony is that each blamed themselves for *not* doing what the other *did*![10]

The point is this, even if we could go back and do what we blame ourselves for doing or not doing, it may not have changed the outcome. It took me so long to breathe in this truth and own it, and I pray in time you too will be able to do the same. Freedom will come as we accept what we cannot change and realize we did the best we could at the time.

When I'm working with a client who is carrying guilt or shame, I want to acknowledge it and help them process it by saying something like "I know there is a *part* of you that feels responsible for the suicide." I don't try to talk them out of the guilt or shame because they need to discuss it to make sense of it. I sit with them as long as it's necessary to help them process those thoughts and feelings. Thinking of yourself in parts is a helpful way to see this.

Just imagine a large circle. Divide it up into pieces, like you would slice a pie. Don't think of your entire circle as being full of guilt/shame, think of a slice of it as holding the guilt/shame, even if that slice seems to be taking up the most room in the pie right now. We know that piece is there, but is there room in the pie for a slice of self-compassion? Even if it's small?[11] In another chapter, we'll work on growing self-compassion, but for now, just be curious if you can offer a little bit of self-kindness to yourself in your own suffering.

After we've processed this guilt/shame (this may take a while),

I introduce the concept of *possibility*. I ask my client to *consider* the idea that the suicide *wasn't* their fault. Then I ask them to sit with that and see what comes up in their body. Remember, we're always drawing attention to the body as well as the mind. What might the body feel like if you were able to let go of this crushing belief?

That's where I start. I'm planting a seed. Something for them to simply consider. If they can consider that there was nothing they could have done to stop the suicide, I proceed by asking them what that would mean for them. How would that look and feel? Then we talk about that. I encourage you to do the same thing. Be curious about these questions and journal your answers.

Next, I'd like you to journal the answers to the following questions:

1. How often does shame show up in your internal monologue?
2. How is shame connected to the suicide or traumatic event in your life?
3. How does shame affect the way you're living?
4. How is shame affecting your connection to others?
5. In what story are you living: the past or present? What conclusions have you drawn about yourself?

Shame walks side by side with its companion, depression. Both grow through silence and isolation, extinguishing the light within that makes us our authentic selves and allows us to feel most fully alive. When who we once were is only a shadow of how we now see ourselves, the only option is to construct a new identity to tolerate being alive. All of this is driven by the collateral damage done to us by the suicide and everything else that follows.

Somewhere along the line, we realize that in order to survive how others see us (stigma), we have to fake it. It's way too painful to be our authentic selves, so we create an imposter (a false self) and begin the charade of hiding and pretending we're fine. It works for a while, yet we often wonder how the heck nobody sees that we're "faking fine." This only exacerbates our sense of aloneness, convincing us all the more that to reach out means we'll be incinerated.

So, what do we do? We start by exploring the myths and lies we've bought into over a lifetime about how to handle pain.

MYTHS ABOUT GRIEVING

Consider as you walk through this grief experience how you learned to handle pain and loss. Again, this goes back to your family of origin. If you grew up in a family that didn't show emotion, or you didn't talk about things like death or loss, it's likely that you learned to stuff your feelings.

You may believe that it's not okay to talk about your loved one's suicide or that you have to be strong and pull yourself up by your bootstraps. You may believe something like a suicide is private and not to be shared. If you've spent a lifetime dissociating from your feelings, you may not even be connected to how you feel.

If that's true, it may be hard for you to even put words to what you feel because you never developed that skill. If that's true, for no real fault of your own, you have censured any conversations from taking place about your grief and thus shut the door to a powerful part of the healing process. Family rules can often be a huge roadblock for the griever. These are the unspoken themes in the family system (e.g., children should be seen and not heard) that were established verbally or through parental behaviors. Dad or Mom made these rules apparent through how they did life.

For example, if you grew up in a family where feelings weren't talked about, or people were met with a wall of silence when they tried to share their feelings, chances are that's how you learned to deal with emotions. Perhaps your parents had marital problems and they didn't communicate. You didn't want to be a burden on the already strained family system, so you avoided feelings or denied there were problems altogether. You learned silence was golden.

Many clients I've counseled over the years have said one or both parents would label them a "drama queen" simply because they expressed strong emotions. Because they felt shamed for expressing emotions, in time they learned to stop sharing and pull inward. Many learned there would be consequences if family rules were broken. (Questions in this chapter's "Consider This" section will help you unpack all this.)

The rules you learned about how to handle grief may be doing you more harm than good. Just know this: the normal response to loss is grief, and grief is something you have to go *through*. It's good to cry. It's good to talk about what you're feeling. Remember, you bury feelings alive only to have to uncover them later.

EXERCISES

Navigating the Storm

We've established that mourning for a death by suicide is a different kind of grief. To help you begin to put words to your pain, I'd like you to conceptualize the following scenario: Imagine being adrift on a small boat and navigating your way through a raging storm. To get to where you need to, you have to navigate through the unchartered waters of *uncertainty.*

You'll be following a map and stopping at several destinations designed to help give you the time and the words necessary to process your pain. Remember that when you've been hit with this type of trauma, access to language often becomes impaired, leaving you feeling all the more isolated and misunderstood.

There isn't any set timetable for this journey, and the companions you will take with you will seem the most unwelcome ones of sadness and suffering. If you're willing, and if you allow them to be your teachers, in time, they will show you a great deal about who you really are and help you reground yourself within new sustainable frameworks of meaning. Only you can make this journey, and only you can decide when you will leave one destination and move to the next.

The first stop is the Dead Sea, aptly named because no life can survive there. As a suicide loss survivor, once the shock wears off, it's normal to feel more dead than alive, as if even the simplest parts of you have been detached from who you once were. Hope lies on some distant shore that is barely visible from the boat and anything and everything you've tried to do to assuage your pain fails. The space between moments feels like an eternity and living has become unbearable.

Below is a list of words. See if you connect with any of them, and write your feelings, thoughts, and beliefs about each of them in your journal.

Terror
Drowning
Isolation
Breathlessness
Annihilation
Depression
Nothingness
Emptiness

The next stop is the Dark Sea. This sea got its name because during the winter, violent storms rocked the water, making it turn a dark color. Suicide leaves the survivor shrouded in the darkness of the blackest night, with the dawn being your only reminder that you're breathing but living in a darkness you didn't cause.

Write about each of these words as they apply:

Panic
Brokenness
Anxiety

Darkness
Fear
Pressure
Confusion
Helplessness

Next on the journey is Poverty Bay. Here, as your rational thinking brain (prefrontal cortex) comes back online, you become acutely
aware that life as you once knew it will never be again. To survive,
you have to create a new normal; but before that's possible, you must
grieve what once was. Poverty for the griever can be defined by the
following words:

Deficit
Inadequacy
Limitedness
Scarcity
Bareness
Uncertainty

So many times along this journey, you may feel tempted to jump
overboard, believing it's just not worth the struggle to survive. The
cords of depression and darkness are doing their best to choke the life
from you. Yet, something deep within you begins to stir, beckoning
you to move forward, and you forge ahead toward your last stop.

The storm is calming now, and you begin to emerge from behind
the shadows. In time, a glimmer of light shines through the darkness
and you find yourself in the Bright Sea, where you begin to think
hope is actually possible. You've learned some valuable lessons from
loss, but more importantly, you've come to know yourself in a way
you never dreamed was possible. You see yourself not through the
clouded lens of brokenness, but through the lens of authenticity, and
you begin to accept each aspect of yourself with compassion.

We see our progress as grievers slowly, perhaps because we've had to begin the painstaking task of creating a new self without our loved one. Sorrow and sadness have been our companions for so long, we've actually become used to their company; but if we allow them, they'll teach us life's most valuable lessons.

My daughter once asked me if I had known all those years ago that her father would take his life, would I still have married him? "Without question," I told her. The love we shared together shaped our lives and made us who we were. It was an eternal love that doesn't end when the recipient is no longer visibly present. It goes on shaping generations to come and can be witnessed daily in the lives of the people it touched. This brings enormous comfort.

So, the great lesson is this: love is a risk without any guarantees, one that we take willingly because its joys far outweigh its sorrows. Love is granted to us for a time, and if that love is fully consuming, there is no greater gift we can receive, but no greater tragedy for us when it ends.

As devastating as your loss is, you won't be destroyed by it, nor will you be defined by it. The grief is still there; it always will be, but you'll just find a place to put it. There will be in the days, months, and years ahead many times you may revisit your pain, but it won't be the same. Over time, the landscape will change, and you'll be able to experience both the sadness and gratitude simultaneously.

Consider the words below, and if you're not ready to write about them right now, save them for a later time:

Expectant
Hopeful
Grateful

Consider This

1. How was grief handled in your family of origin?

2. What beliefs about dealing with grief did you assimilate
    from your family?

3. What myths have you bought into about how to handle
    grief? For example:

    It's not okay to cry.
    I should handle my grief alone.
    Others won't want to be around me if I'm sad.
    I need to be strong.
    Family business is private.
    Others don't want to hear about your problems.
    I need to replace the loss.

4. Do you find it easy or difficult to express your emotions?

5. Answer the following T or F questions below. Journal your
    reasoning behind these answers. The answers will tell you a
    lot about how you're currently handling your grief.

    I believe people should grieve alone.
    I believe you should try to replace a loss.
    I believe you should keep busy and distract yourself, so you
       won't be sad.
    I believe that when you're sad, it's normal to express it.

I believe my loved one wouldn't want me to express sadness.

I believe there is shame associated with my loved one's suicide.

I believe others will feel uncomfortable around me because of the suicide.

I believe people don't really care to hear about my loss.

6. As you consider the possibility of your loved one's death not being your fault, think back to the Remembered Resource Person exercise. Go through those steps again. Be aware of the responses of your body and mind. Then, record your thoughts in your journal.

Stigma is a big roadblock to sharing about suicide. Know this: things won't change in our families, our schools, our places of worship, or our society, until we begin to talk about these most difficult issues. Vulnerability is the key to eradicating shame. Let's start the conversation!

Chapter 6

Stigma

"This [disease of mental illness] comes with a package . . . a real sense of shame. . . . How come every other organ in your body can get sick and you get sympathy, except the brain?"

—Ruby Wax[1]

After WWI, soldiers were stigmatized for being weak because of symptoms doctors and the general public couldn't understand. How could a man be a war hero and then come back exhibiting symptoms of amnesia, hysteria, and the inability to communicate?

In 1915, an English physician, Charles Myers wrote the first paper to describe this phenomenon he called "shell shock." He theorized that the symptoms these soldiers were experiencing were the result of constant exposure to concussive blasts, which caused brain trauma. Unfortunately, his theory didn't hold up. There were plenty of soldiers who were experiencing these symptoms who had not been exposed to these blasts and still experienced symptoms.[2]

The *medical* community came to view this idea of shell shock as *weakness.*

Soldiers were archetypically heroic and strong. When they came home unable to speak, walk or remember, with no physical reason for those shortcomings, the only possible explanation was personal weakness. Treatment methods were based on the idea that the soldier who had entered into war as a hero was now behaving as a coward and needed to be snapped out of it.[3]

It wasn't until Abram Kardiner wrote *The Traumatic Neuroses of War* that perceptions began to shift. Kardiner suggested that the symptoms veterans were experiencing were psychological in nature rather than cowardice or character flaws. These people *couldn't* just snap out of it as was once believed, and in fact, these symptoms could last anywhere between six to twenty years (remember there was no effective treatment then), if they ever disappeared at all.[4]

Fast forward to WWII, the Korean War, and Vietnam, which only saw an increase in symptomatology from returning vets. And, today, we know a great deal more about the brain and how exposure to things like sexual assault, child abuse, a traumatic loss, or any cataclysmic event can lead a person to develop PTSD. For veterans, the statistics are pretty staggering with about 17.6 individuals committing suicide each day in 2018.[5] This leaves behind a lot of survivors, and as we've seen, survivors of suicide loss are at a high risk for PTSD and for taking their own lives.

CONFUSION

If someone has cancer or a broken bone, the visible symptoms can be seen and therefore more easily understood. The most difficult thing about a suicide, a mental health disorder, or the experience of a survivor is that people don't understand the etiology, or cause. They haven't been educated about what happens in the brain of someone who is clinically depressed or severely anxious or has experienced a traumatic event. Therefore, it's easy for people to think that these folks should be able to just "snap out of" these states.

Unfortunately, when things go awry in the brain, other people can't always tell. They certainly can't see it, so they can marginalize those who have these disorders. All this leads to fear and social isolation for the individuals who are suffering. This is the last thing *these* folks need.

The church in particular has historically handled the topic of mental illness with little understanding and has therefore missed the mark, causing many people a great deal of added pain. Ideas that mental illness can be prayed away, that depression is all in the mind, or that people who commit suicide are eternally lost have only served to demoralize, shame, and hurt those who suffer with mental illness and those who live with them, love them, and may be left behind to mourn them.

Stigma confronts individuals with one word: shame. They feel marginalized by society, often condemned by family and friends, and shut down to their own sense of self. People can feel shame for all sorts of reasons, for things they've done, things they've failed to do, or who they intrinsically are. I'm certainly not suggesting that everyone who carries shame will experience suicidal thoughts. However, those individuals who struggle with a mental illness or suicidal ideation have, according to research, been shown to avoid seeking help from a mental health provider.

Let's take a look at some different types of stigma in the hope that if you're dealing with any of this, we can shed some light and truth on your pain and confusion.

SOCIAL STIGMA

The state of Montana has historically held the highest rate of suicides in the United States since 1999. What were the possible causes?

> Factors exacerbating the distressingly high suicide rate in Montana include long, dark winters, a stoic "cowboy up" mentality, lack of mental health awareness, and social isolation. This lethal combination not only contributes to suicidal ideation and behavior, but to a precursor factor—stigma.[6]

Stigma is not a new concept, although with the dramatic increase in mental illness and suicide it has received a great deal more attention in recent years. This particular study was interested in finding solutions to stigma against suicidal ideation and help-seeking behavior (in Montana). Three primary mechanisms explain how stigma contributes to suicide and to survivors of suicide loss.

First, according to the stress-coping model of stigma (originally published as a scholarly paper, *Schizophrenia Research*[7]), stigma is a *social stressor* that promotes "'negative emotional reactions, social withdrawal, and hopelessness among people with mental illness, especially if the perceived threat of stigma and social rejection exceeds the coping resources of the individual.'"[8]

Stigma also "'contributes to the *social isolation* of a person experiencing a mental health problem, in part by discouraging interaction and a *sense of belonging with others.*'"[9] Sound familiar? (See Ehlers and Clark's research and Joiner's model in chapter 2.) In turn, the social isolation may contribute to the risk of suicide because it causes the person to avoid discussing their mental health with other people.

Finally, "community-wide stigma is associated with individual self-stigma," a stigma an individual imposes on him or herself. "Studies on predictors of help-seeking have shown that both public stigma and self-stigma are associated with lower willingness to seek help for mental health problems."[10]

This was true with my client Kendal, who came to my office a number of years ago after having a breakdown. She told me she never would have come for therapy if things hadn't become so bad. Her mother had taken her life when Kendal was twenty-five. Now Kendal, at 35, had started to experience panic attacks and severe depression. She reported that she never dealt with the suicide and had started using alcohol as a way to cope.

Kendal had a set-in-stone belief that one should always handle their own problems and that "shrinks" were for "crazies." I asked her where that belief came from, and she said her father. Her mom was anxious and depressed for most of Kendal's life, and she had shunned therapy because her husband didn't believe in it. After the suicide, it made sense that Kendal didn't get help, but continued buying into the myth that you must handle your own problems and do so in silence.

As time went on, Kendal became increasingly anxious and depressed. She tried reaching out to a few people but was met with the wall of silence. "People just didn't know what to say," she told me, "and those who did listen eventually got tired of hearing about it." She felt marginalized in her workplace as well and said that when she'd pass people in the hallway, they would look the other way so as not to have to talk to her.

Her boyfriend even broke up with her, saying he feared mental illness ran in her family and he was scared to commit. Kendal was totally broken. Her life had pretty much shut down. That's when her mom's sister reached out to her and encouraged her to get help. We talked a lot in our work about how stigma marginalizes survivors and how their feelings of shame and inadequacy often lead them to turn inward and self-blame.

Kendal's beliefs about seeking help were passed down from her father, as well as the Asian cultural beliefs about mental illness and suicide that she grew up with. In her father's generation, having a mental illness cast shame on the entire family, therefore, it was kept hidden while victims suffered in silence.

I worked with Kendal for a couple years, and she made a powerful transformation. She was able to refute many of the myths she grew up with about mental health, and she learned to find her own voice to speak up about these issues and the stigma surrounding them. This is the only way things will change. Let's look more closely at how different types of stigma develop, and as we go through this, see if any of this hits home for you.

SELF-STIGMA

Self-stigma is a process whereby stigmatized individuals perceive themselves as social outcasts. Many have experienced situations where they have been marginalized, discriminated against, or felt shamed in response to the negative attitudes of others toward mental illness. All this serves to create a poor self-image for the individual, ultimately leading them to internalize the stigma and shut down.

Individuals who hold the belief that they are a burden to others may also believe they will be ostracized by others. Additionally, the negative beliefs they hold about themselves will perpetuate avoidant behavior. In the quantitative studies, 15 percent to 35 percent of participants indicated that they had concealed their loss experience or did not want to talk about the death for fear of being judged or misunderstood.[11] I found this to be true after a couple years went by. I could tell the people in my life who just didn't want to hear about it anymore. They thought I was doing well and that I should just focus on moving forward. To avoid judgment, I just kept quiet and hid the pain.

Community-wide stigma is also associated with individual self-stigma. Studies on predictors of seeking help have shown that both public stigma and self-stigma are associated with lower willingness to seek help for mental health problems.[12]

Have you ever read, heard, or had someone say something like this to you?

"Suicide is such a selfish act; it is cowardly, and I can't believe they would do that to their family . . ."

I can't tell you how many people have said that to me or around me. It's painful to hear. I understand their thinking, but it suggests that our loved ones operated with a mind that could choose wisely. They were sick; it's as simple as that. If the sentiment above is what the average person in the community believes, it's easy to see why people don't want to seek help.

Perhaps your loved one refused to get treatment. Perhaps they were afraid of being judged or misunderstood. I know Mike was. Understanding all this has given me greater compassion for what my husband was suffering, as well as what I've suffered as a survivor. Truth be told, before I became a therapist, I was probably one of the people who would have agreed that suicide was a selfish act. That's why it's important to speak out and educate those in your sphere of influence about mental illness.

Suicide loss survivors can be hit hard by social stigma, thereby leading to self-stigma. Many survivors react with concealment and social withdrawal to perceived and internalized stigma, fearful of sharing with others about their loved one's death. I felt as if I had to hide Mike's condition from people because of his position in the community as a dentist. I didn't want to do or say anything that would jeopardize his practice. I was trying to honor his wishes that we keep silent; in the end I sorely regret that decision.

This happened to a former client I'll call Sally. Her husband was diagnosed with bipolar disorder and she lived through years of emotional suffering with his illness. He was unstable and oftentimes out of control when he'd go off his medication, which Sally reported he did often in the early years. Things had been going pretty well for quite a while once they found a combination of drugs to stabilize him.

Sally never told anyone about his illness. He wouldn't allow it. He felt embarrassed and ashamed. So she, like many of us who deal with those who suffer with a mental health issue, stayed silent, telling no one except her mother that he had contemplated suicide. One day, her husband left work and never returned home. It was only then that she reached out to family. Sally's husband ended his life and left her to deal with the enormity of guilt she felt for trying to protect him from the stigma he so greatly feared from his family, and from his workplace.

Another way stigma can be experienced by survivors is by the violation of their privacy. We've seen this a lot with the many celebrities who have lost their lives to suicide over the last few years. We've also been privy to their personal and private information that has been broadcast all over the media.

It's difficult enough to face the aftermath of a loved one's death by suicide, but to have your private family information on display for the entire world to see is demoralizing. While most survivors aren't celebrities, we too can be victims of gossip and the spreading of information that we've perhaps shared in confidence.

My husband was a respected member of the community, and I'm sure all sorts of gossip circulated about him after this tragedy. Most people were genuinely concerned; others just wanted to know the gory details. I know people were talking about me as well. It's not only humiliating for a survivor, but so dishonoring to the memory of their lost loved one.

Finally, we want to dispel the notion that just because someone is struggling with a mental health issue, that doesn't mean they will always end their life. No one can totally understand the complexity of reasons for why a person chose to end their life, but we can learn how to better address the topic of mental illness in our culture. Consider how stigma has affected you as you have walked through your loved one's death thus far.

THE CULTURE

Another topic to consider when we talk about stigma is the idea of how the culture you're living in, or grew up in, views mental illness and suicide. Remember, since WWI the medical community looked at post-traumatic stress as weakness. Many of these cultural beliefs die a slow death, just like we saw with my client Kendal. That's why teaching people about the causes, symptoms, and treatment of any mental health issue is crucial.

In some cultures and religious doctrines, suicide was and is thought to be the unpardonable sin. This idea had its theological roots in the early teachings of St. Augustine in his treatise, City of God. When Rome was pillaged by the Germans in 410 CE, many Roman Christian women were raped. Augustine wrote to remove their defilement because they hadn't had consensual sex. However, when a woman named Lucretia took her own life in response to the rape, Augustine's response was that she had committed a greater sin against God because of her suicide.[13]

During the tenure of Pope John Paul II in the 1990s, the Catechism of the Catholic Church acknowledged, for the first time, that:

> . . . grave psychological disturbances, anguish, or grave fear of hardship, suffering, or torture can diminish the responsibility of the one committing suicide [and that] we should not despair of the eternal salvation of persons who have taken their own lives. By ways known to him alone, God can provide the opportunity for repentance.[14]

What are some of the reasons religious institutions held these affirmations? Because it was and still is believed by some that the person who died by suicide had no time for repentance, and therefore, their act is unpardonable. Yet many deaths occur without the opportunity for the person to seek forgiveness for any sin—for example, the soldier who was killed suddenly by a grenade or the person whose mind has succumbed to Alzheimer's disease.

The truth is, no one can assume that they know the final thoughts of a person who was in such mental despair. Maybe many of these broken souls did cry out to God and ask for mercy and forgiveness for what they were about to do.

THE WALL OF SILENCE

I was speaking at a world conference for the American Association of Christian Counselors with speaker and author Natalie Ford. We were presenting on suicide. Her husband had also taken his life several years prior. Her part of the presentation touched on stigma, and she shared some messages that were written to her following her husband's death that were hard to believe.

Natalie received a number of Mass cards from friends saying they were praying that God would rescue her husband from hell. She recalled how painful it was to hear that and how it only added to her feelings of shame.

> A lot of the stigma I faced was perceived . . . I thought people blamed me (and maybe they did) and I didn't want to go out in public because I thought everyone was whispering about how pitiful it was that I lost my husband to suicide.[15]

Several months after my husband died, my friend Patty Jo suggested I join a suicide loss group and a grief group. The grief group was held at the church I was attending and, although most of the people in the group lost their loved ones to cancer, I thought it was still a way to meet other widows, some of whom are friends today.

I was invited to a luncheon by the woman who was leading the group. She was also a widow. She wanted to introduce me to some other widows in the church. While we were all settling in, someone asked how my husband died. When I said that he had died by suicide, one of the ladies literally screamed aloud and jumped out of her chair. I don't think she was trying to be mean in any way; she was just shocked and unprepared as to how to deal with me.

Many times, when we share that a loved one died by suicide, we are met with a wall of silence because people don't know what to do or say. This was also something that happened in the women's Bible study I was attending at the church. I was asked to share my story because I was the new person coming into the study. No one jumped out of her chair this time, but in all those months of attending, not one person asked me how I was doing or reached out to me. The silence was painful. The good news is that while some people didn't respond in the way I had hoped, I always felt the presence of God and that was what ultimately carried me.

Silence can also happen in the family system. For many survivors, the silence begins with the loved one who took their life. As I mentioned in chapter 3, many people are stunned that their loved one was in such emotional pain, or even considered suicide because their loved ones erected a wall of silence themselves.

Consider the invisible agony our loved ones were carrying and how that, combined with the terror of staying alive and being silent, contributed to their deciding that physical death would be a welcome relief to the emotional death they were living.

Many families, especially in years past, didn't ever speak of suicide, especially to their children. In the book *Silent Grief: Living in the Wake of Suicide*, Christopher Lukas makes a strong case for the damage done to survivors because of the wall of silence. Lukas, the survivor of multiple suicides in his family of origin, didn't learn his mother committed suicide until he was sixteen. His father told him as they sat at the train station waiting for him to leave for college—no explanation, nothing about her illness (manic depression), just *your mother killed herself*. Lukas had no idea why his mother took her life, and he spent years trying to answer the why questions and find healing. He was left to tell his brother, who later died by suicide. Prior to that, his aunt and uncle had also taken their lives.

In my suicide loss group, I heard many such stories, like the woman who shared she was fifty years old before her mother told her that her father had committed suicide. She was devastated, spending years thereafter feeling isolated and alone. The good news, if there can be any, is that because suicide has dramatically escalated in the past few years, the wall of silence seems to be falling. The media is even being responsive by airing programs and publishing articles to get the message out that we need to understand, discuss the topic openly, and educate the culture about mental health.

WHAT DID YOU JUST SAY?

The other problem survivors face is the influx of opinions and comments others often make. Well-meaning friends tried to get me to "move on" after the first year. This made me feel even more guilt about not moving forward quickly enough. Remember, I believed I had caused my husband's death and now I couldn't even do the grief thing right! I was drowning, until one day, my friend, who is also a therapist, sent me a Facebook post written by Kay Warren, on the first anniversary of her son's suicide in 2013.

> Here's my plea: Please don't ever tell someone to be grateful for what they have left until they've had a chance to mourn what they've lost. . . . The truest friends and "helpers" are those who wait for the griever to emerge from the darkness that swallowed them alive without growing afraid, anxious, or impatient. They don't pressure their friend to be the old familiar person they're used to; they're willing to accept that things are different, embrace the now-scarred one they love, and are confident that their compassionate, non-demanding presence is the surest expression of God's mercy to their suffering friend.[16]

Warren's Facebook post was a game changer for me personally, and I passed it on to others to help them understand the brevity of the grief journey, the difference a death by suicide engenders, and the patience that is required from friends and loved ones as the griever struggles to move forward.

If you are walking alongside someone who has lost a loved one to suicide, do your due diligence. Your loved one doesn't need you to say something profound, they just need your love and understanding. The touch of a hand, a hug, or your own tears for the pain they are experiencing speaks volumes. Sometimes your loved one may not even need words, just your presence. Just allow them to be where they are and love them until some light reaches into the darkness they're living in.

EXERCISES

Surrender: Cultivating an Attitude of Willingness

What do we as survivors do when we're met with a wall of silence or stigma? We surrender. Let me explain what I *don't* mean by surrender. We don't give up. We don't go with the status quo. We don't *not* stand up for ourselves. We don't become victims. Surrender is actually the most empowering way to live our lives, and I'll tell you why: once we surrender the things we can't control, they no longer have the power to drag us down.

So, what is surrender then? It involves giving over a *right*. A right is something we demand from ourselves, God, or other people. Rights say things like this:

I must have things be a certain way in order for me to feel okay.
I have to understand why my loved one took their life.
I must have others like me.
I have to have others' approval.
I can't experience rejection.
I must be understood.
I shouldn't have to forgive those who hurt me.

For me, living from an attitude of surrender means I can rest knowing God is in control and He is using events, other people, and the circumstances I find myself in, to change me and help me grow. Surrender is really about moving toward "acceptance." If you can't change something, you can either fight against it, which I believe is fighting the wrong battle because we are using all our emotional energy only to find we achieve the same miserable outcome. Or, you accept whatever (or whomever) you're struggling with and focus on the things you can actually do something about. That looks like taking all that emotional energy to brainstorm possibilities within our control and problem solving.

Why do we demand rights in the first place? Because it gives us a measure of control. It also helps us avoid the uncomfortable feelings of pain and rejection we don't want to experience. The truth is, we're going to experience them anyway; the question is, will it be with an attitude of resignation or relinquishment? When I'm operating from an attitude of resignation, I'm stomping my feet, furrowing my brow, and clenching my teeth saying "Okay, fine, I'll surrender the right to be understood!" Relinquishment looks like holding my hands and heart open, letting go of any and all expectations and saying, "I'm willing to be misunderstood and trust God with the rest."

At some point in life, we come to the realization that others are going to disappoint us, we are going to disappoint ourselves, and God doesn't seem to be doing too much about all the things that are upsetting the apple cart. Why? He wants us to depend on Him, and because His heart for us is to live in freedom. And freedom means surrendering our rights to *His* will and plan, even if we don't understand it right now.

For us as survivors, that may mean surrendering the right to know the whys about our loved one's suicide. That doesn't mean we don't ask all the questions and do all the meaning-making work. It just means that after a while, we need to let it go because, we may *never* have all the answers. Freedom is living in the assurance that *God* knows.

Consider This

Here are a few of the beliefs I held, the rights I had to surrender, and the things I had to learn to trust God with over time. I want to help you unpack the same things for yourself. If you're not ready yet, that's fine. Simply save this section for later or skip it altogether. Make your own surrender list using mine as a guide if you like. Remember, surrender is simply cultivating an attitude of *willingness* to let go of the things we can't control anyway.

Rita's Surrender List

Belief: I must have others understand I did everything I could for Mike, or I will be undone.

I will surrender: The right to be understood.

What I'm willing to experience: I'm willing to experience being misunderstood by others and live with the anxiety that creates for me.

Belief: I have to know why Mike would leave me.

I will surrender: The right to know and to have all my questions answered.

What I'm willing to experience: Sadness.

Belief: I must have Mike to be secure.

I will surrender: The right to have Mike be my security.

What I'm willing to experience: I'm willing to experience that anxiety that goes along with being without him.

Belief: I have to have people understand how shattering this was for me.

I will surrender: The right to have people understand how I feel and to have them say all the right things in the way I would prefer them said.

What I'm willing to experience: I'm willing to experience the aloneness this creates because no one but God can really understand my pain.

Whether we're dealing with stigma, with people who say insensitive things, or perhaps even people who blame us, we have to be willing to experience all the discomfort that goes along with that or we'll find ourselves doing all sorts of crazy things behaviorally to make ourselves acceptable and understood. Just like my friend Natalie, who isolated herself to avoid the perceived whispers, remarks, and shame that surround her husband's suicide, we too will experience more turmoil and grief trying to hold on to our rights to be understood.

Use the surrender chart below to record any rights you may need to surrender now. Feel free to refer to mine above.

BELIEF	I SURRENDER THE RIGHT TO . . .	I'M WILLING TO EXPERIENCE . . .

Chapter 7

Existential Shattering

"We were under great pressure, far beyond our ability to endure, so that we despaired of life itself. Indeed, we felt we had received the sentence of death."

–2 Corinthians 1:8–9

"When you're going through hell, keep going."[1]

As I will reiterate throughout this book, a traumatic event shatters the core foundational beliefs in our lives that make the world safe and predictable. Emotional trauma brings us face to face with our own inadequacy and threatens our very existence on every level of life. As you know, an event like losing a loved one to suicide will radically impact what you believe about life, God, and the world around you. So, let's explore this idea of existential shattering and try to work our way toward establishing new sustainable frameworks of meaning.

The idea of an Existential Shattering (ES) was first developed by psychologist Tom Greening through his teaching and presentations. The development in the scholarly literature emerged as students and colleagues began applying and researching this concept. What is it exactly? Here's how Greening defines it: "Existential shattering is the sudden and unexpected dismantling, or shattering, of one's self-conception and worldview as a consequence of an event or process that the individual has experienced."[2]

An additional description notes a "devastating, unexpected,

irreversible event, a trauma, in which one's fundamental systems of meaning and relating are *irreparably* shattered"[3] (italics mine).

There is, however, a difference between existential shattering and post-traumatic stress. According to the findings, the defining feature of both ES and PTS is not the actual event or what happened; it is the underlying *effect* of the event, or how the person *experiences* the event.[4]

Although most often triggered by trauma, existential shattering is not the same as PTS. The latter emphasizes "trauma and stress" while the former is concerned with the "enduring irrevocable destruction of one's former ground of being."[5]

In other words, it is possible for one person to experience a traumatic event and develop PTS without any signs of ES, while another person might experience the same event and experience one, or both.

The real questions to be answered are, how does the person see themselves, God, and the world around them *after* the shattering event? Is the world a safe place? Can they trust others? Can they trust themselves? Will others be there if they are needed?

The first defining factor of ES is that the event was sudden, unexpected, and irreversible, all of which are true in a suicide. Secondly, the event must have caused a severe disruption to the person's meaning and relating (to self and their world construct). It was once believed that a person who experiences existential shattering will not be the same person ever again. They will see themselves differently, and they will see the world differently. It's true we won't be the same people again, but it doesn't mean we can't be different and better.

The third defining factor is that the event forces confrontation of one or more of the person's *set-in-stone beliefs about* existence. The world can become a meaningless place where many of us who once felt grounded and secure are left questioning our very existence after a traumatic event. We have experienced a shattering that brings with it questions we already thought we had the answers to. While older theories of ES focused primarily on negative aspects, newer research notes that if faced, there is a potential for benefit and opportunity, and, I would add, potential for post-traumatic growth after the suicide.

Fourth, the event leaves the person feeling groundless. Spiritually, people may have questions like, *Is God good? Can God be trusted again? Is suicide unforgivable?* All this brings people to a crisis of faith. According to Hoffman and Vallejos, "a person might be left questioning or leaving a religious group they have associated with for most of their life and without that familiar ground, feel lost, without anchor or lacking solid ground."[6]

Finally, the shattering event causes a person a sense of disillusionment with a formerly held or cherished belief. Suicide loss leads survivors questioning the very foundations on which their lives were built.

The apostle Paul certainly captured the level of despair a human being can experience when he wrote, "We were under great pressure, far beyond our ability to endure, so that we despaired even of life itself. Indeed, we felt we had received the sentence of death" (2 Cor. 1:8–9). As survivors, pressure, or unexpected shattering, produces an enormous burden on the soul. A burden we don't believe we can bear, leading us to believe we don't have the ability to endure life without our loved one. The fractured soul can leave us despairing of life, feeling the sentence of death in own lives. The good news is that the shattering from this traumatic event does not have to be irreversible or irreparable.

Why? Paul answers this question in the next passage:

But this happened that we might not rely on ourselves but on *God* who raises the dead. He has delivered *us from such a deadly peril, and he will deliver us again.* On him we have set our hope that he will continue to deliver us. (2 Cor.1:9–10)

God's answer to the unspeakable shattering I experienced was Himself. He was the hope Paul talked about. That's how Paul was able to go on, and that's how I was able to go on. I took that hope and eventually used it to help others, and I believe that's why I didn't give in to despair. That's the point, using our stories to reach back and strengthen others who are suffering.

Making our way through the shattering is lonely business, and others can't always be there to comfort us or walk alongside. Even if they are, they can't be in our skin and feel the depths of our pain. So, we're left alone, terrified as we figure out all the mess that remains and doing so without the anchoring presence of our loved one to make the world feel more secure. We feel adrift, lost in a world that doesn't make sense anymore.

When we're feeling hard-pressed on every side and feeling as if the life is being choked out of us, we come face to face with the hard questions the shattering brings up. We can't sit on the sidelines with these questions because every belief we anchor ourselves to at this juncture will affect our entire life trajectory. We have to get down and dirty with the issues of life.

Where does all this leave us? Deciding . . . about everything. And deciding will take a while as we process what's happened to us. Your love one's suicide has not only affected you, but it has affected everything you once believed.

BUILDING A NEW SUSTAINABLE FRAMEWORK OF MEANING

In order to inch our way to new and sustainable frameworks of meaning, we must build a strong support network to sustain us. The first step could be seeking help from a trained therapist who can offer their attuned compassionate presence in a place where you can feel safe enough to discuss the most intimate details of the shattering. You may feel embarrassed or ashamed that you're questioning everything about your life and faith, so you need a safe person to do this work with.

The idea of meeting with a therapist may cause resistance. I understand. There is a push-pull effect here. You want someone to confide in so that you can unload, but you simultaneously recoil at the idea of the telling to protect yourself and maybe even your loved one. You may feel you're betraying them if you say anything negative. If this makes sense to you, stop and ask yourself what role the resistance is serving in your life. Be curious about what story the behavior is trying to tell.

I obviously had no problem going to a therapist, but I was protective of Mike's image (stigma). I didn't want to say or have anyone else say anything bad about him given the way he died.

It's also important for you as survivor to be able to move in and out of the depths of your emotional experience, as well as your thoughts. In this way, you don't get stuck in either place, which in the initial stages of grief is difficult. Gently moving back and forth between thoughts and feelings allows you to do what we therapists call "emotional processing." In this process, you will over time be able to gradually rebuild your worldview and your sense of self.[7]

EXERCISES

"Navigating the Storm" was an exercise to help you begin to put words to your pain and do some of this emotional processing. Let's do another exercise that will help you delve a little deeper into your now existing belief system.

Shattered Vase Exercise[8]

This is an exercise I like to do with my clients because it helps them put words to the shattering. I show them the image of a broken vase from the cover of my book *Shattered* (it can be an image of any shattered object). See if the exercise is helpful to you too.

Study the image below for a moment. In your journal or notebook, write a few statements that describe what you're feeling about your life when you look at the image. In the box beside the image below, I've listed some of the things I've said, as well as what others have said. These statements become a segue to digging deeper into the emotional pain and belief systems we're holding.

A bomb went off in my life
My life has no meaning
I'm responsible for . . .
My life is in ruins
I don't know who I am
The world is a scary place
I have no reason to live
Life will never make sense again

Many times, people are in such shock and denial after a suicide, they can't even process what's happened. It seems unreal on so many levels. I didn't want to even entertain the idea that I could go on, or that I could build a life without Mike. Instead, I wanted to put all the broken pieces of the vase back together the way it was, but that wasn't possible. In order to heal, I had to first move to a place of acceptance about what happened, while still holding the pain.

My heart for my clients, and for you the reader, is to help you honor the broken pieces of your lives and take those pieces and create something new, something that can still be beautiful and meaningful in the future.

Once we figure out how the suicide has changed your beliefs, you can begin to challenge some of the assumptions and work your way to that new framework of meaning. Let me show you how to begin this process using the Dysfunctional Thought Record.

Toxic Thought Record

I know I sound like a broken record, but beliefs are the most powerful things we choose. They drive our behavior on the subconscious level. I'm going to illustrate my beliefs using a worksheet I call the Toxic Thought Record (TTR). This is based on an adapted and expanded version of the Dysfunctional Thought Record developed by a pioneer in the field of psychotherapy, Aaron Beck and his colleagues.[9]

I use the exercise regularly to help clients understand how their toxic thoughts are contributing to their misery. (You will have the opportunity to create your own Toxic Thought Record with the worksheet in the appendix.)

To begin this process, I'd like to have you look at some *thinking errors* we are all prone to make in life. Therapists call these cognitive distortions. (I wrote a whole book on this titled *Think This Not That*.) Let's just look at a few of these cognitive distortions to see how they play into our belief systems and contribute to the despair we oftentimes feel.

Cognitive Distortions

All or Nothing Thinking
You see things in black and white and there are no shades of grey. Things are either perfect or a failure.

Jumping to Conclusions/Mind Reading
I assume my belief is an already established fact without checking out the evidence.

Catastrophizing
You attribute the worst possible outcome to a situation or event.

Personalizing
You see *everything* as your fault or about you.

Emotional Reasoning
You make your feelings into facts. *I feel bad, so I am bad.*

Negative, Self-Defeating Thinking
Your default is to dwell on negative thoughts that cause you pain and turmoil. Instead, ask yourself is there another way of thinking about this situation or problem that will help you move forward.

Now let's look at some ways to challenge these thoughts through the practice of Socratic questioning. With this method you're going to be challenging thoughts and beliefs by asking yourself questions that stimulate critical thinking. Burn these questions into your brain so that you can call them up in the moment to challenge your irrational beliefs.

1. What evidence do I have to support this belief? Could there be an alternative explanation for what I'm believing?
2. Is there another way to look at this situation, or this belief, that would be equally valid and get me what I want?
3. What evidence might refute this belief?
4. What would an impartial observer or friend say about what I'm thinking or believing?
5. What's the worst that can happen to me, compared to what I've already been through?
6. How can I use my strengths to deal with the worst-case scenario?
7. Is there a better way for me to think about this situation?
8. Is this, the way I'm thinking, always true in all situations?

Go to the appendix and start filling out the Toxic Thought Record for yourself. You can use mine as a guide if you like. Below, I've unpacked it using these tools.

RITA'S TOXIC THOUGHT RECORD		
Situation	**Beliefs**	**Feelings**
Mike takes his life.	I can't live without him.	terrified, anxious
I'm alone.	I won't make it w/ out Mike.	fearful, insecure
I stayed in Florida.	I'm responsible for his death.	intense guilt, despair
People talking.	I must have people understand.	anxiety, depression, fear

Remember I told you that I was an anxious child? This wasn't because my parents were unavailable for me, but because of how my brain was wired (all the genetic stuff we talked about earlier). I'm bringing this up again to point you to my beliefs in the middle column above. Next, look at my feelings on the right side of the chart. Now, take a look at the diagram below. I've expanded the Toxic Thought Record to include my past.

TOXIC THOUGHT RECORD

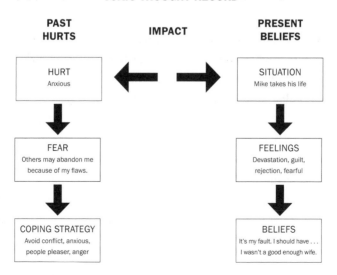

If you look, you'll see that from a young age, I held an uncon-
scious belief that others might abandon me because of my flaws. I
feared rejection. To deal with all that, I developed some ways to cope:
try harder, be a people pleaser, and avoid conflict. That way, I could
control (to some degree) whether others would reject me. When
my husband took his life, it was the most radical form of feeling
abandoned. Even though I know he wasn't in his right mind, on a
feelings level it felt like he had abandoned me.

When someone who is a people pleaser feels that others aren't
pleased with them, they experience a certain amount of anxiety. If
you look at my thought record in the chart, it's easy to see why I fell
prey to feeling as if I caused Mike's death.

Look at the cognitive distortion list earlier in the chapter, and see
if you can identify all the thinking errors I made. As you go through
your own thought record, look at what distortions in thinking you
may be making, then use the list of Socratic questions to challenge
those distortions.

Here are the cognitive distortions I was making: *personalizing*,
using *emotional reasoning*, and *catastrophizing*. Personalizing, in that
I wasn't willing to look at Mike's part in this event. It wasn't *all* my
fault. Emotional reasoning, in that I was believing I was bad. I caused
this. Catastrophizing, because I believed with every fiber of my being,
I couldn't live in a world without him in it.

I'm not trying to minimize my shattering or suggest that for a
given period of time it wasn't okay for me to feel as if I couldn't live
without Mike, but as I was able to challenge that belief, as well as
the others, I came to see I *was* living without Mike. I'm not saying
I was happy, but I was doing what I had to do and moving forward
to sustain these new frameworks of meaning.

I was trying my best to acclimate to a new normal. I was able
to acknowledge his part and I was able to see that I wasn't a horrible
person. I was human, and I made some mistakes, but I didn't *cause*
him to pull that trigger. It was his choice alone.

As you make your way through your list, you may see and understand that how you feel about your loved one's suicide may not just be connected to how you feel now in the moment. These feelings may also be connected to your past, contributing to some of your negative self-defeating thinking. The past always has an impact on the present, and we have to look back to examine that impact if we're going to try to build a new framework for our lives.

We've seen that suicide brings us to a crisis of belief and a crisis of faith and because of that, many of us will be angry. Some of us will be angry at God. So, what do we do about Him and the anger we may feel toward Him? Certainly, there are no easy answers, but I can tell you this from my experience through this oftentimes unbearable darkness: I would never have discovered that God was all I needed, until He was all that I had. Just as we began the journey of deciding about other core areas in our lives, we also have to decide where we'll land with our faith. Let's press on and talk about it!

Consider This

1. What cognitive distortions are you making? Are you able to challenge them? If not, what's keeping you stuck?

2. What emotions and beliefs have you identified that you are willing to address now?

3. What was it like doing the Shattered Vase exercise? What were some of the sentences you wrote down? Which is the most difficult to live with?

4. Are you angry at God? How has your loved one's suicide shattered formerly held cherished beliefs?

5. Are you at a place now that you can work on these issues, or do you need more time to process?

Chapter 8

Unfinished Business

"Forget the former things; do not dwell on the past.
See, I am doing a new thing! Now it springs up; do you not perceive it?
I am making a way in the wilderness and streams in the wasteland."

–Isaiah 43:18-19

At the beginning of the book, we talked about some of the why questions people struggle with after suicide loss. We didn't, however, address the why questions as they relate to God, so let's dig in. I think a good place to start is being honest about our feelings about God after such a tragic event has occurred in our lives. I've counseled many people who feel it's not okay to be angry at God. I assure you that your anger is no surprise to God, so we might as well get it out in the open.

If you're angry with God, use the TTR (toxic thought record) to express the situations, feelings, and beliefs you're now holding. If you don't have faith in the God of the Bible. If you don't adhere to any particular faith persuasion, or if you don't believe there is a God, I only ask that you be curious about how holding those beliefs sustain you after such a significant loss.

This section is about your being curious about wherever you're at with whatever beliefs you hold. You can certainly skip this section too if it doesn't feel right. If you'd like to move ahead, you'll find some questions to ponder in the "Consider This" section at the end of this chapter. Take time to reflect on them and answer them honestly.

The forces coming against you want nothing more than to take out your faith. If that happens, it cuts off a lifeline for you. I don't believe God *causes* bad things to happen, but it's evident that He doesn't always prevent them either.

I'm reminded of the movie *God's Not Dead* where Josh Wheaton, a Christian, enrolls in a philosophy class at his university taught by Professor Jeffrey Radisson, an atheist. On the first day of class, Radisson demands that his students sign a declaration that "God is dead" to get a passing grade. Josh refuses to sign the form and is challenged by Radisson to debate the topic of God's existence in front of his fellow students to avoid being expelled from the class.

In their last debate, Josh asks Radisson the question, "Why do you hate God?" After Josh repeats the question twice more, Radisson explodes in rage, confirming he hates God for letting his mother die, leaving him alone despite all his prayers for her healing.[1] There you have it. There's always a story behind those raw emotions we feel; and there are always belief systems driving those feelings. If a supposedly good God doesn't answer a prayer for healing for a loved one, it's easy to see how a person can turn on Him with fury.

The enigma of suffering is messy business. It's seems so unfair that some people go through so much and others seem to have so much less to bear. So, who's to blame? Who is to blame for my husband's suicide? For your loved one's? Is it God? Is it the devil? Or is it fate? My go-to search for some answers about suffering is the book of Job in the Bible. For those of you who aren't familiar with it, you may want to read the story. I'll set it up for you here:

Job was an upright, God-fearing man. Satan, God's adversary, entered the courts of heaven to petition God to allow him to bring calamity into Job's life. This wasn't just a simple trial for Job, it was total annihilation. All his kids died, all his possessions were destroyed, and his body was stricken with sores and boils. In the midst of all this, his wife (who also suffered shattering loss) urges him to curse God and die. Through all of this, Job remains upright and doesn't curse God. He did do one thing: he brought his complaint (lament) before God.

What if, like in the book of Job, Satan approached God in the courts of heaven with a pitch to annihilate my life, and it went something like this: "Rita only worships You because she has a good life. Rita has Mike. He's everything to her; take him away and she will curse You to Your face."

Could it be a test? It was for Job. In Job, the story and the test had far reaching implications. Maybe this story of Job is in the Bible so that we could all learn from it centuries later. The point is this: Job, although boldly honest, didn't sin by charging God with wrongdoing (Job 1:22), and, in the end, God restored all Job had and more.

God had His reasons for allowing Satan to test Job, but Job also had free will in choosing how to respond to the test. If we're talking about our loved one's suicide, we have to factor in two other things—free will and possible mental illness. I could suggest that the choices Mike made, and didn't make, about treating his depression led everything to spin out of control. My husband got to choose how he responded to the trial he was obviously living in, but it wasn't God's choice.

I prayed continually along with many others for God to protect Mike. That didn't happen. Or did it? I could contend that maybe it did. Maybe, had he lived in the state he was in, things could have become much worse. I could also argue that mental illness is a by-product of a fallen world.

During the three months Mike was showing signs of illness, he could have followed through with the act, but it was thwarted for one reason or another. So, I could argue for the positive and believe I was granted a gift. Even amidst the chaos of those months, I was able to talk to Mike and have deep conversations. I learned some things he never told anyone, not even me; things that were deeply troubling his soul. I was able to gain understanding, which, in the long run, has helped give me some closure. I was also able to see how much Mike loved and needed me. During that time, he also went to a treatment center. Four months after he died, I found his intake form and read the incredible things he wrote about me. All of that helped with alleviating my guilt.

The point, however, is this: Mike died. I didn't get the happy ending I wanted, and neither did you. I didn't curse God, but I did go through a period later where I was angry with Him for a lot of other things that resulted from the suicide. There were many times when I said, "Okay, God, when is enough, enough? I'm tired, I'm weary, and I'm undone by all these trials. How much do I have to go through before the trials cease to strengthen my faith and begin to chip away at it?" You may feel the same.

As time has unfolded, I have learned a lot about who God is. I came to that understanding the way I always have: by seeking after Him with all my heart. I read my Bible. I meditated on specific verses that comforted me, and I poured out my lament before Him, begging for comfort and assurance. God gave me assurances that helped me heal some deep wounds. He was the same God who showed up for me over and over through the countless trails I faced in the past.

The story isn't over—not for you or for me. The real story may just be unfolding. I am more certain than ever that God often allows what He hates to accomplish a greater plan and purpose. We aren't always guaranteed the happily-ever-after endings we want in this life. What we are guaranteed is God's *presence* in the midst of tragedy. I pray in time you can draw comfort from that.

LAMENT

What actually is a lament? It's a deep and passionate expression of grief. I like to use the Psalms in the Bible because they are raw, but beautiful expressions of grief concerning the issues of life. Feel free to use whatever resources you have to do this. You may have another resource or practices to use.

In biblical times, the Psalms were the hymnbook for the Hebrew people. Most were composed by King David as he found himself in the crucible of suffering. The Psalms almost always tell a story. If you use this idea, you will be using your story, and you will bring it boldly and honestly before God. What I love about the Psalms is how they pierce the heart. Making no pretense, David directs his desperate cries to God using powerful verbiage:

> I am poured out like water,
>   and all my bones are out of joint.
> My heart has turned to wax;
>   it has melted within me.
> My mouth is dried up like a potsherd,
>   and my tongue sticks to the roof of my mouth;
>   you lay me in the dust of death.
> (Ps. 22:14–15)

The Psalms also deconstruct our often-held tacit assumptions that we were meant to have a trouble-free life. This is part of the great dilemma we face in the existential shattering. Not to trivialize, but bad things do happen, even to people who have checked all the right boxes. Trials and suffering don't always come with a rule book or a nice, neat explanation.

The Psalms also show us that evil happens not just because people make bad choices, or don't have enough faith, but because we live in a fallen world where injustice surrounds us.

When we feel betrayed by our loved one for leaving and maybe even by God who is supposed to love us beyond our comprehension, it can make us not only feel anger, but a profound sense of being adrift without an anchor.

We can try to put on the mask with God and pretend, but He wants entrance into the parts we're ashamed to admit. Acknowledging and confessing our anger at Him for the pain we feel does a couple things: First, it allows us to feel *something* when our hearts feel mostly numb and dead. Second, pouring ourselves out "like water" before

God means we're actually *doing relationship*. If you love someone, you tell them the deepest and most scandalous things in your soul. If you always stay silent, how do you have a relationship or grow through adversity?

After we express our anger, we might actually feel better because we've opened our hearts to God and have been authentic with ourselves. The Psalms also help us to put language to the ripped pieces of our soul, so don't allow guilt to sidetrack you from being honest with God.

In the Psalms, we see plenty of people being unfairly accused, misunderstood, angry, and betrayed. We can resonate when David says he was betrayed by his close companion in Psalm 55. In short, we see ourselves in these verses, and we tap into our own sad tale as we meditate on them. These Psalms weren't written by people who had it all together. To put it in today's vernacular, they were a hot mess.

If we've learned anything from our tragedies, it's that life is full of different seasons, light and darkness. And when we walk the valleys of sorrow and suffering, we shouldn't be surprised. The good news is that God isn't afraid to enter the darkness with us, and He'll keep going there with us for as long as we need Him too.

I read the Psalms all the time after Mike took his life, because in those pages, I connected with Mike (he loved the book of Psalms) and with God. In those times, God didn't take away my pain, and He hasn't erased it from my life, but as I tell Him about the horror of that day, I feel He understands, and He wants to comfort me. One day, He's promised to make all things new. One day, I'll be with my beloved again.

Below are some of my favorite Psalms. If you'd like to try this, focus on one a week. As you read each one, take time to pause and reflect on the words and record what it brings up for you personally.

Psalm 13
Psalm 18

Psalm 22

Psalm 27

Psalm 42

Psalm 51

Psalm 55

Psalm 91

The following story birthed the famous hymn, "It Is Well with My Soul." This song of lament has touched many of us throughout the years. Horatio Spafford wrote the famous hymn after the deaths of his four daughters. Here's his story:

> In 1873, to benefit his wife's health, Spafford planned an extended stay in Europe for his family. At the last moment Spafford was detained by real estate business, but Anna and the four girls sailed to Paris on the steamer *Ville du Havre*. Within twelve minutes on November 21, 1873, the luxury steamer sank in the middle of the Atlantic Ocean after being rammed by the British iron sailing ship the *Lochearn*.

He received a telegram from his wife Anna that she alone had been saved.

> After receiving Anna's telegram, Horatio immediately left Chicago to bring his wife home. On the Atlantic crossing, the captain of his ship called Horatio to his cabin to tell him that they were passing over the spot where his four daughters had perished. He wrote to Rachel, his wife's half-sister, "On Thursday last we passed over the spot where she went down, in mid-ocean, the waters three miles deep. But I do not think of our dear ones there. They are safe, folded, the dear lambs."
>
> Horatio wrote this hymn, still sung today, as he passed over their watery grave.[2]

If you've never heard this song, I encourage you to find it online and listen. See what comes up for you as you ponder the lyrics. Is it anger? Sadness? Disbelief that someone could write such words after such traumatic loss? Record any insights in your journal.

IS SUICIDE UNFORGIVABLE?

We touched on this subject briefly in an earlier chapter, but I'd like to dig a little deeper because this is one of greatest causes of angst for survivors of suicide loss. Let me ask you to read the following imaginary scenario:

> Matt was a great guy and beloved by all. Good husband. Good father. Loved his career. Committed to his faith and his family. But for some reason, not entirely clear to him at the time, Matt became very depressed and anxious. Perhaps he had some kind of chemical imbalance in his brain. As time passed, he fell deeper and deeper into a web of despair, and he was unable to function. Others noticed a huge change in him. This once vibrant, charismatic man was now withdrawn, a shadow of his former self. Matt couldn't even go to work; he became increasingly paranoid. His wife threatened to leave him if he didn't get help, and he found himself feeling more and more isolated and alone. This went on for two years. Matt finally decided to heed his wife and doctor's advice and go into treatment. Right before he was to leave home and while his wife was out, Matt took his life to end his pain.

What do you feel for Matt? Sit with this for a minute. What was your answer? My guess is, it was probably to show mercy to Matt. What do you think God would do with Matt? Condemn him for eternity, or embrace him into heaven? In the Bible, a thief was crucified next to Jesus. He had lived an entire life of sin and only repented here in the last moments of his life. Yet did God condemn him? No, just the opposite. Jesus told him that on that very day, when his life ended, he would be with Jesus in paradise.

As a Christian, I believe what's most important to God as we walk out this life, and what determines our eternal destiny, is our response to Jesus' gracious offer to rescue us from ourselves and make us true children of God. God is love. It's His very essence, not just a character trait, so if love and mercy are God's essence, why would He condemn one of His children who had a sick and tormented mind to eternal damnation because of the way that person died? I don't for a minute believe that God called Mike home by way of suicide, but I do believe He *welcomed* him home. Our loved ones were in a mortal battle against themselves, motivated to be freed from unbearable anguish and many suffering from mental and or emotional illness.

Author Albert Hsu explains this battle in light of God's love in his book *Grieving a Suicide*:

> The motif of tragedy compels us to understand our loved one's final act in the context of the full story of his or her life. In the tragedy of suicide, our loved ones fought against an enemy within. They lost their battle against themselves. While part of them may well deserve God's judgment, another part may well receive God's mercy.[3]

Look again at Hsu's analogy of suicide as a tragedy. A tragedy by definition is the sorrowful or terrible events encountered or caused by a heroic individual. I've mentioned that my husband played the role of hero in many people's lives, often to a fault. Hsu sheds light on this by looking at literature:

> In literary terms, a tragedy is the story of a tragic protagonist who is undone by a fatal flaw. "Often the tragic hero comes to a moment of perception, usually an insight into what he or she

has done wrong to set the forces of retribution in motion. As the tragic plot unfolds, the tragic hero becomes gradually isolated from others. Tragedies typically end with the death of the hero."[4]

Perhaps your loved one fits into this category. Perhaps not. I know Mike did, and his flaws gave me insight as to how this could have happened. These illustrations helped me put to rest the idea that suicide is unpardonable. I pray they will help you too.

EXERCISES

Lament Exercises

Write a lament of your own to express your grief. A lament includes a complaint, a confession, and an indication of trust in God and His intervention.

Phototherapy

Create a collage of photos, magazine pictures, and even objects that help illustrate your lament.

Poem of Lament

If you were to write a poem of lament, what would you title it? What would the theme of the poem be? How might it help your grief journey?

Making Music

If you're musically inclined, write a song or melody of lament.

Finish the Sentence

You may want to use these sentences to describe where you are at different stages of your journey. They will help you to identify your fears and your beliefs and give you insight into what you may want to focus on in your work.

This is a story about . . .

The most difficult thing about it is . . .

The thing I am most afraid of is . . .

The thing that will help get me through this is . . .

The way I want to see this story unfold is . . .

How I see myself at the end of this story is . . .

Consider This

1. Do you believe that God is punishing you for something related to your loved one's suicide?

2. If you answered yes to the above question, how has that belief affected your concept of God?

3. Do you struggle with believing suicide is an unforgivable act? Why or why not?

4. Do you think losing your loved one is some kind of test for you? Explain.

5. If you read the story of Job in the Bible, what were your thoughts about how God tested him? Could that help you in any way? Explain.

6. Do you believe trials make you stronger? If so, what have you seen in yourself with regard to the suffering you've endured?

7. How did you feel reading the story about Matt? What came up for you?

8. What conclusions if any have you drawn about suffering as you've walked through this journey?

9. Where will you run for comfort?

Chapter 9

Making Peace with Ourselves

"This is a moment of suffering. Suffering is part of life. May I be kind to myself in this moment. May I give myself the compassion I need."
—Kristin Neff[1]

"Kindness is the language the deaf can hear and the blind can see."
—Christian Nestell Bovee[2]

Compassion is a curious thing. If you look it up in a thesaurus, you'll see words like mercy, kindhearted, empathy, and concern to name a few. I always thought I was a pretty compassionate person; my chosen profession is somewhat of an indicator of that I suppose. I feel intensely for people's sufferings, I empathize with their situations, and I find I want to encourage and reassure them that in the end, things will be okay. If I can do all that for others, what makes it so hard to do it for myself?

One word: *self*-compassion. It's a totally different beast, and one we aren't particularly good at in our culture. I see it in my clients all the time. They can be so loving, giving, and kind to everyone else, but when it comes to showing some mercy on themselves, they can't do it. In fact, they do the exact opposite; they beat themselves up with a strong inner critic I call the "judger." Maybe you're familiar with this voice; I know I was. So how do we tackle this, and how do we learn to show ourselves the compassion we so desperately need in this time? Glad you asked.

In chapter 7, I provided a list of Socratic questions to challenge your self-defeating beliefs. One of the questions on that list is important as we look at the idea of self-compassion. It's one of the three central tenants of Kristen Neff's research on self-compassion that we'll look at. Neff is recognized as an expert on self-compassion. The first in her triad is *be kind to yourself*.[3] So, if you continually berate yourself, instead ask yourself this question from that list: *What would I tell a friend who was thinking or saying this?* Chances are, you'd encourage your friend to be kinder to themselves.

You probably wouldn't tell your friend not to feel a certain way, but instead encourage them to tell you more about what they're feeling, maybe offering a reassuring touch or a kind word. You wouldn't dismiss them. You'd probably remind them that they did their best and they aren't perfect (something my friends did daily for me as I berated myself). That means, according to Neff, realizing that being human means we're subject to *limitations*.[4]

In order to do all this, you have to *notice* how you're treating yourself. You have to pay attention to your *self-talk*. You have to intentionally practice loving kindness and patience with yourself, and you need to do it with an attitude of acceptance and curiosity as opposed to judgment. This is Neff's third key component of self-compassion: *mindful awareness*.[5] This type of awareness involves observing your thoughts without reacting harshly. We never want to deny or avoid our feelings; we want to notice them and put words to them as we learned in an earlier chapter.

When I'm working with a client in session and I notice their language is negative or self-defeating, I may pause and point it out, asking them if there is kinder, less judgmental way they can speak to themselves, a way that will help them move forward and get them what they need. When I would start tearing myself to shreds about being responsible for Mike's death, my friend Patty Jo would say,

"Rita, you loved Mike till he took his last breath. I will listen to anything you need to talk about, but I won't listen to you blaming yourself." It really helped.

Spend a day intentionally observing your self-talk. See how many times a day you're speaking negatively to yourself and pay attention to how it affects your mood and overall sense of well-being. If you're carrying guilt about your loved one's suicide, chances are you have some negative self-talk going on.

Remember, shame and guilt are relevant predicators of self-criticism. This negative self-talk can create a cycle of self-destructive behaviors as well as more toxic negative self-talk. You can practice self-compassion. If you do it daily, your brain will learn to default to the new normal because you've strengthened the muscle of self-compassion.

Think about what happens in your brain this way: if you're skiing down a mountain that's covered in virgin snow, you'll make a pathway on your first run. If you ski repeatedly down that exact spot on the slope, you'll create a worn pathway. You have to do the opposite of what you normally do (self-criticize) to create a sustainable new pathway (self-compassion).

FINDING SELF-COMPASSION THROUGH PARTS:
THE GOOD, BAD, AND UGLY

Richard Schwartz, another pioneer in the field of psychotherapy, developed a model in the 1980s he called Internal Family Systems (IFS). The model posits that each individual possesses in the mind a variety of sub-personalities, or *parts*, that work to protect the self.[6] For example, you could have an angry part, a judger part, an anxious part, and a compassionate part, to name a few.

Schwartz noticed that most of the clients he saw in his clinical practice couldn't distance themselves from these negative internal monologues that played repeatedly in their minds from different parts. In his approach, Schwartz found a way to help clients identify these voices and understand their role and function.

In this way, parts could be understood and given space to express themselves: good, bad, and ugly. Recall some of the feelings I mentioned that you might experience during this journey as a survivor, including depression, anxiety, fear, and emptiness. There are other parts too: happy, funny, compassionate, and curious. Parts are simply whatever comprise who you are and how you see yourself—all different expressions of you.

The inner critic many of us deal with is also a part of you, one that can often have a louder voice after a loved one commits suicide, and these parts all need to be validated for the protective roles they play in our lives. In short, they need a voice. Let me give you an example of what this might look like using an illustrative client I'll call Karen.

Karen came into my office several years ago because she discovered her son had taken his life in their home. After some time had gone by, Karen realized that she was angry, and she wasn't sure why. She was very close to her son, and she didn't feel like her anger was directed at him, but she knew something was keeping her stuck.

As I got to know Karen, it became apparent to me that she was angry, but the anger was turned inward. I talked to her about seeing herself in parts and asked her to envision those parts as slices in a large pie-shaped circle. One of the slices was a loyal part of her that was trying to do the job of protecting her from allowing this angry part to come forward and express how it felt.

Why? Because in Karen's mind, if she said anything bad about her son or was angry with him, it meant she was a bad mother and didn't love her son. She needed to protect her son's reputation and be there for him at all costs, even if it was to her own detriment.

I asked Karen if she could focus on this loyal part and find it in her body. She sensed a tightness in her gut. I asked her how she felt toward this part, and to my surprise she said she hated it. Karen shared that for as long as she could remember, she had been a people pleaser who did everything others expected of her without expressing her true feelings. She didn't know how to draw good boundaries because she was afraid to be rejected. She did this with her son too, not wanting to upset him because he was emotionally fragile.

I asked Karen if she could find some compassion for this loyal part of herself, knowing that it was trying to protect her from the overwhelming feelings of anger that might be released if she ever found her voice. She told me that she was afraid if she showed this part compassion it would keep ruining her life, and she would never find her voice. I assured her that by being curious about this loyal part, she might gain insight on what this part wanted her to know.

As she accessed this part of herself, she reported that it was tired of playing the role of peacemaker and pleaser. It was tired of her being a doormat and never speaking up. It was tired of being fearful of being rejected by others. There was shame tied to this part too because of a secret she carried regarding her son. She couldn't afford to let anyone know the truth for fear of shattering the "perfect image" she had created about him.

We also discovered that the angry part of Karen had been there much longer than she was initially aware of. It was angry at all the wrongs she swallowed for years in the name of doing the right thing. It was most angry at what her son had done. The loyal part of her kept this angry part under wraps so she wouldn't have to face fallout if she told her family and friends what had really happened.

As Karen got to know this angry part of herself, she was able to see that it wasn't such a threat. It wanted to protect her by keeping her from being overwhelmed with emotions she couldn't deal with. As we validated the loyal part of her for being a good mother and a compassionate person, that part began to soften. It agreed that it would step back and allow the angry part of her to have a voice.

Once a client understands that the their real/authentic self is capable of managing other more unwelcome parts (anger), they will often relax and step back. Understand here that because Karen viewed anger as unacceptable and loyalty as being a good person, it was hard for her to access the anger she held.

I asked Karen to talk to this loyal part of herself and assure it that she was capable of managing her anger without its protection. She asked this loyal part if it would be willing to step back long enough to see what the angry part wanted to say. Karen found her loyal part was willing to relax a bit in order to get fully in touch with the angry part of herself.

When we engage the various parts of ourselves and become curious about why they are doing what they're doing, we generally find we are led back to one or more pivotal events, oftentimes traumatic, that have shaped those parts and their need to protect us.

In Karen's case, once her angry part revealed the secret, it was easy to see how the trauma of that event in both her life and her son's led to her anger. Because her son had taken his life, Karen didn't feel the freedom to access the anger because she was so overcome with grief. Once she was able to dissect the parts of herself and tease out what they were each believing, she was able to show each part of herself compassion for what she had endured. This didn't happen overnight, but in time, Karen was able to access her anger toward her son and forgive him.

WHAT SELF-COMPASSION IS NOT

"I've never been one to feel sorry for myself," Karen said stoically. "I remember my mom always drilling into me that the world didn't revolve around me. 'Other people have worse problems than you,' she would say. You didn't whine or complain in our house." Karen learned to equate self-compassion with *self-pity*, a mistake many people make.

When people self-pity, they are self-absorbed, and they tend to personalize suffering as being only about them; they give no real thought to others. They also have trouble stepping back and looking at their suffering from a global perspective. In other words, they're always wrapped up in their own drama, clueless of the fact that suffering is common to humanity.

Yes, there are times in your life and in this journey of recovery where you will feel self-pity. I think you deserve a few of those moments; your life has been decimated. To be labeled as a "self-pitying" person, however, you would have to act this way all the time. You'd have a victim mentality.

Karen, by her very nature, was a pleaser, always doing for others, maybe sometimes resenting it, but doing it, nonetheless. She was far from a victim. She thought more along the lines of "What I'm going through is very difficult, but others are going through suffering too, maybe worse scenarios than mine."

Self-compassion, according to Neff's research, is not *self-indulgence*.[7] This was why Karen was afraid of her loyal part and didn't want to give her angry part a voice. She was worried that if she showed compassion to this loyal part, it would let her get away with anything. She wrestled with herself constantly about the secret she was keeping about her son. Her loyal part was telling her it was okay to not speak up, just indulge your son and protect him at all costs no matter what he's done.

A simple example of self-indulgence would be this: every time you feel stressed out, you stay home from work, go shopping, and buy yourself new clothes, then you go home, watch television, and eat a whole bag of Oreo cookies. That is not a good way to care for yourself if you're doing that on a regular basis. Again, keep in mind we're talking about a consistent way of living here.

If you're worried you're going to become self-indulgent, think about your core values, and ask yourself if your life has been a reflection those values. If you believe you're moving toward health and well-being and exhibiting behaviors that are congruent with your values, chances are you aren't being self-indulgent. Caring for oneself is an opportunity to rest, refresh, grow, and be who you're designed to be.

Many people use their inner judger to goad themselves into change or action. This approach may work for a while, but if we actually believe the harsh things we say to ourselves, the negative effects of that will take their toll. By continually shaming yourself, you may find that you lose faith in your abilities altogether.

Having self-compassion is not about making excuses for things you don't like about yourself or want to change. For lasting change to occur, you have to be honest with yourself and face the behaviors that are incongruent with your core values. In that way, you'll keep self-pity and self-indulgence at bay.

The last thing Neff's research shows is the difference between self-compassion and *self-esteem*. As a survivor, there may be things you're struggling with that have affected your self-esteem. You may see yourself as a bad person, or someone who made an unforgiveable mistake, lowering your sense of self-worth. But self-compassion isn't about self-worth, or how much we accomplish so we can finally value ourselves; it's about realizing that common humanity deserves understanding, care and compassion just because we are human and created in God's image.[8]

Unless we can come to understand and appropriate our intrinsic worth through God's eyes, beyond our performance, we'll always be looking to gain approval from someone or something because self-esteem develops and grows in direct proportion to our achievements and successes. Self-compassion develops by growing the inner traits of patience, kindness, and gentleness with ourselves. It begs the questions "What really matters to me?" and "What kind of person do I want to be?" It allows us to turn back when we've made a mistake and own it by acknowledging it and apologizing. We don't have to berate ourselves in order to be forgiven.

Like resilience, self-compassion can be learned and practiced. Neff states:

In a surprising twist, the nurturing power of self-compassion is now being illuminated by the matter-of-fact, tough-minded methods of empirical science, and a growing body of research literature is demonstrating conclusively that self-compassion is not only central to mental health, but can be enriched through learning and practice, just like so many other good habits.[9]

Now let's take look at how to put all this into practice.

EXERCISES

How to Be Kind to Yourself

Where do you start, and how do you learn to show yourself compassion? Use all the tools you've learned so far in this book. There are many things we've talked about that you can implement in this practice; you just have to be intentional to do them, or it won't work. The more energy you put into these exercises the greater payoff you'll find. Here are some reminders and some new ideas to try.

- Practice mindful awareness.
- Remember to slow things down.
- Do deep breathing and relaxation.
- Notice your judging thoughts.
- Reframe the judging thoughts using positive affirmations.
- Practice gratitude.
- Realize you're human and subject to limitations.
- Practice soothing behaviors (warm bath, reading, writing, music, art, dance, nature).
- Do something nice for yourself (get a massage, soak your feet, get a manicure, go to the beach or mountains).
- Do something nice for someone else.
- Repeat a positive affirmation about yourself out loud.
- Wink at yourself in the mirror or give yourself a hug.

- Write a letter to yourself from the perspective of your deceased loved one, a parent, best friend, or God. Include all the things this person sees in you—weaknesses, strengths, and all. Then read the letter out loud to yourself.
- Write a letter to yourself from your loved one who died. What would he or she want to say about you? Read it out loud to yourself.
- Come up with three statements (beliefs) that you hold that say something positive about you. Say them out loud for one minute. See how that feels (as opposed to negative self-talk).

Consider This

1. Is it hard for you to show compassion to yourself? If so, why?

2. What beliefs are behind your answer to the above question?

3. How does it feel to think you are human and subject to limitations? Does it help? If not, why not?

4. Have you spent time practicing mindful awareness? If so, what changes have you noticed about how you view yourself? Has it made you kinder to yourself?

5. How do you feel when you think about the sufferings of others? That suffering is universal and you are not alone in it?

6. What is one thing you could tell yourself to feel validated with regard to your feelings?

7. What is one thing you could do for your body, mind, and spirit to feel physically soothed?

Chapter 10

Facing the
Dark Side

*"In your anger do not sin: Do not let the sun go down
while you are still angry."*
—Ephesians 4:26

Whether you're angry at God, angry at yourself, angry at others, or angry at your loved one, you have to do something with those super-charged feelings, or they will eat you alive. Your anger is actually a useful thing; it's trying to tell you that something is going on in your soul that needs tending in order to experience the peace and rest you were designed to live in. Think of it like the warning light that comes on in your car when something is wrong. You can ignore it, but eventually, if you don't fix what's wrong, it will cost you.

Anger is a secondary emotion, which means it sits on top of more vulnerable emotions. Surprisingly, I explain it to my clients by using a giant, plastic M&M I have in my office.

The hard candy shell of the M&M represents anger—the kind I *show* others because it protects me from more hurt. What's inside when you bite through the hard candy shell? The soft chocolate. That represents the more vulnerable emotions I *don't* show others for fear of rejection—things like sadness, hurt, abandonment, shame, guilt, and rejection.

Anger is a natural emotion. There is nothing wrong with feeling anger, it's what we do with it that can become problematic. Why? Because anger can keep you from healing. It will sit beneath the conscious surface and gnaw at your soul, making it impossible for you to have peace or closure.

The first step in dealing with anger is to recognize it. Own it as being your own and your responsibility. You may not be ready to forgive the people who hurt you just yet, but in order to heal, you need to process the feelings and beliefs that go with the anger. That means you have to talk about it. To help you begin that process, I'm providing you with a tool later in the chapter called the Debt Document. (The Debt Document is available in the appendix at the end of the book.)

First, take a minute and ask yourself how anger shows up in your life. Do you stuff it down inside? Do you explode? Do you deny it? Do you do a slow burn? Do you seek revenge? Do you hide it? Remember, in order to deal with anger, you must first be honest about it with yourself and uncover the meaning you've attached to it.

Start paying attention to where you feel the anger in your body. What sensations do you notice? Where are they located? Do you tense up? Do you notice your heart starts beating faster? All these are signal that your body is getting activated. Next, pay attention to what you tell yourself in those moments when the anger surfaces. Do your thoughts help to escalate your anger or cause you to stuff it down and bury it? Are you ashamed or fearful of expressing your anger, like Karen in the previous chapter? If so, identify the beliefs attached to it (i.e., *I'm not allowed to show anger*, or *I have to be right and make my point*).

SHATTERED DREAMS

Anger can be the result of a blocked goal, a hurt, or a perceived loss that elicits a response such as *I got what I didn't want, and I wanted what I didn't get.* In the case of survivors of suicide loss, the anger is the result of a concrete loss—death by suicide. That means there will be a shattering from the death and a great deal more shattering from all the unmet desires and expectations that follow.

In the next section, we'll work on the Debt Document, but before we do, think about your relationships from the past. This is a good time to use your Toxic Thought Record. Each survivor has a different story of pain, some stories beginning far before your loved one took their life. This pain, be it from your childhood or your adult life, carries with it an attachment wound.

This wound may have laid dormant in your soul for decades; even so, it has impacted your belief system and how you've learned to love and be loved. Why is this important? Because if these wounds from your past have created anger, and that has gone unresolved, it will add fuel to the fire of your current situation.

Let's use Karen again as an example. Karen had always been a pleaser and a conflict avoider. Her loyal part would call her a doormat. Flipping the pages back on Karen's life revealed more to her story. Karen's parents divorced when she was eight, an event that devastated her. She idolized her father, who left his family for another woman. Karen wanted her dad's approval and did whatever she could to get it. As time went on, her dad spent less and less time with her, causing her to feel all the more abandoned.

By the time she was in college, she barely heard from him. Karen, being the pleaser and conflict avoider that she was, turned her anger inward, blaming herself. She was a disappointment, a failure, and a bad daughter. To cope with all these feelings of inadequacy, Karen turned to food. This was a huge source of comfort for her—a friend who wouldn't leave or disappoint her.

Karen never resolved the anger with her father and didn't connect the dots as to how buried anger sits quietly, sometimes for decades, until something else catastrophic happens and totally unravels us. Her disappointment with men didn't end with her father. Karen's husband betrayed her, solidifying her already established beliefs that she was unlovable and not good enough.

Karen put all her love, loyalty, and identity into her young son, making him her life. As he grew up without an engaged father, he began having problems. Because Karen couldn't risk losing his love, she placated him and drew no boundaries for his behavior. The boy was troubled, and by the time he was a teen, it became evident that he suffered from a bipolar disorder.

Karen overcompensated for him because he didn't have a good father and because he was always depressed. She was angry, but she didn't dare show it. She was angry at her husband for being so disengaged and leaving her to try to do everything for their son. She was angry at her son for taking advantage of her and angry at her father for starting this mess.

Why am I sharing all this? Because like Karen, we all have a "cardfile" on the people we love. Maybe you have one on your loved one who died or maybe it's on someone else close to you who is connected to the loss. If so, you need to uncover that record so that you can see how it's affected where you are now.

I had to deal with a lot of stuff from people who were supposed to love me in the aftermath of Mike's death. Over the first few years I lost relationships that were important to me. It was extremely hard. I wasn't mad at God about Mike, but a few years later, I realized I was furious about all the other things that happened because of the suicide. If I hadn't unpacked all that, I wouldn't have been able to connect the dots and resolve my anger at God (and significant others) for all the injustices I felt I had incurred.

Take time to think about past hurts and anger (even if it's anger at your loved one) and how these feelings are impacting your current situation and the anger you're experiencing today. It's also important that you see yourself as one of the people you have a relationship with. If you're angry at yourself, unpack the reasons why.

Karen's life wasn't focused and whole until she began to see that her anger started when she was eight and her dad walked out. She was too young to process that loss intellectually and place responsibility on the guilty parties because the pre-frontal cortex (rational brain) isn't developed enough for children to think abstractly; thus,

Karen believed that it was her fault that her dad left. She believed she was unlovable. Until she dealt with that first loss, it would be difficult to connect the rest of the dots in her past.

EXERCISES

The Debt Document

The goal of the Debt Document is to help you forgive someone and can be pulled out of your toolbox when you need it.

To begin, you'll need a sheet of paper. At the top of the page, write the name of the "transgressor," or the person who has offended you. The person can be living or deceased. (You can make a sheet for each person you are angry with; e.g., yourself or someone else). Set it up as you see it below in three separate columns:

TRANSGRESSOR _____

WHAT HAPPENED	WHAT I FELT AND CAME TO BELIEVE	WHAT I LOST

In the "What Happened" column, describe the event(s) that caused your anger at this person. The following items will help you get started:

- What events still stand out in your own mind that you have not forgiven the transgressor for?
- What still causes you to feel activated? These things are good indicators that you haven't forgiven this person.
- Don't list things you feel you have already forgiven this person for, only list what you're still holding a grudge for.

The middle column, "What I Felt and Came to Believe" is where you describe how you felt about the event(s) that happened, and most importantly, what you have come to believe about yourself as a result. Using Karen again as an example, she might have written down the scene of her dad walking out on their family in the What Happened Column. In the middle column, she would explain how that event made her feel. I'd also direct her to identify what she believed about herself as a result of this event. She might respond that she felt rejected, humiliated, discarded, and that she came to believe she was unlovable.

In the "What I Lost" column, write down what you've lost because of what this person did. For Karen, she lost trust in men because of her father's abandonment. If I'm working with a client of faith, I might appeal to their faith in God and ask: "What could you trust God for now because of this loss?" They might respond: "I can trust God to be faithful. I can trust God to be my security."

Once you have completed a list(s) for everyone who has transgressed against you, you'll begin the task of emotionally processing (you'll recall this involves toggling back and forth between thoughts and emotions) each column on that person's document. This simply means you need to process your hurt and pain. You can do that through journaling, or you can discuss your thoughts with someone safe. Do this for each Debt Document.

When I'm leading clients through this exercise, I focus on the beliefs they hold now. Here are some things to consider about your beliefs as you process all your answers:

1. Have your beliefs changed or shifted in any way because of the suicide or other consequences of the event?
2. Do you only hold this belief about yourself (God or others) because of your loved one's suicide?
3. If so, how is this belief different than it was prior to the suicide?

These are just some things to consider as you process the hurts. You don't have to write anything down on the Debt Document, but you will want to reflect on how your beliefs have changed following your loved one's death.

Once you have done all the talking and processing you need to do with documents, you can move on to an exercise called the "empty chair."[1]

Empty Chair Technique[2]

You can do this in the privacy of your own home. Here's how it works:

Sit in one chair with another empty chair facing you. Using your Debt Document as a guide, imagine that the person you've listed as the "transgressor" is sitting in the chair facing you. Again, the person can be living or deceased. Read through the offense in the What Happened column as if you're having a conversation with the person facing you.

Next, you'll explain how what happened made you feel, and what you've come to believe about yourself as a result. Then, you'll state what you feel you lost.

Here's an example:

Dad, it hurt me when you told mom you wanted a divorce and left me standing in the driveway that day to cry and scream and you wouldn't take me with you. I felt unloved, abandoned, and rejected.

I came to believe that I was unlovable, not good enough, and of no value.

I lost years of my life dealing with all the pain.

If you want to do the exercise for your loved one who died, you could say something like this:

[Your loved one's name], it devastated me that you took your
    life and left me.
I felt _____,
    and I have come to believe _____.
I lost _____.

If you're completing a Debt Document about yourself, you can put your own name as the Transgressor.

[Your name], I'm angry at you because you _____.
I felt _____,
    and I have come to believe _____.
I lost _____.

Proceed through the entire document until you've read all the debts out loud. The end point is now an opportunity to grant forgiveness to the offender. This is where you tell that person you have forgiven them, and you have released them from the debt they owe you (real or perceived). They never have to make it up to you or pay you back—they are free.

You are "granting them freedom"; but in truth, you're freeing *yourself* from carrying the burden of unforgiveness that has been suffocating the life from your soul. Below, I provide a script I use for clients that you can follow, but you can say whatever seems right to you. The point is, you're honest with yourself.

Once you go through the entire process with each transgressor, you can shred the document, set it on fire (you can use flash paper to do this safely), or sign and date it as a reminder that you made an event of the exercise and it's done! When I do this in faith-based groups settings, I have people actually nail their document to a small wooden cross. The point is, I have them create a ritual around the forgiving to make it memorable.

Here is an example using details from my experience:

Offender: Mike

What Happened: Mike refused to get help.
Feelings: frustrated, scared, angry
Beliefs: I don't matter enough for you to work on your stuff.
   I'm not worth fighting for.
What I lost: security, love

What Happened: Mike takes his life in our bedroom.
Feelings: horror, shock, abandonment
Beliefs: I am all alone now. I wasn't worth fighting for. I
   wasn't a good wife. I am a terrible person. I will never be
   happy again.
What I lost: security, love, value, acceptance, adequacy

This is a short list, all the things I talked about with my therapist for several years as I worked through this maze of shock, disbelief, and betrayal. As time wore on, I had to admit I was angry and process that part of myself that held it. You must do the same if you want to heal. This process isn't an easy fix, so be patient with yourself.

Use the Debt Document and the Empty Chair Technique anytime you need to process anger. Remember, forgiveness begins with the decision of the will and is born out in the emotions. Once you've decided to forgive, the emotions of love, sympathy, empathy, and compassion will need to be accessed so you can continue to walk in forgiveness. This applies to your loved one and anyone else you need to forgive. You learned how to practice self-compassion in chapter 9, so now give yourself the gift of compassion and be intentional about it.

WHAT HAPPENS NEXT?

Once you've forgiven someone, the logical next question becomes: now what? Does this mean you're reconciled with this person and the relationship is restored? Not necessarily. Let me explain the difference between forgiveness, reconciliation, and restoration. Forgiving someone takes only one person: you. You can forgive someone without their even being a part of the process. This would include your loved one who died.

Reconciliation takes two people: the offender who asks for forgiveness and the wounded person who grants forgiveness. That may or may not occur. The next step is the person who has been wounded deciding if they want to be restored in relationship with the offender. That decision is based on the nature of the relationship. If the offender has historically been abusive, toxic, or a user, you would probably not want to enter into such a relationship again.

If the offender wants to be restored in relationship with the wounded person, it's up to the wounded person to draw appropriate boundaries around the relationship. This is common among family members. Say a parent is an alcoholic and the offended person fears how the exposure to the parent's behavior may affect their children. In this case, it's perfectly appropriate to draw boundaries around the time spent with this parent. Choosing what's best for yourself and your family when moving through difficult life situations requires reflection, boundaries, and prayer for those who pray.

Consider This

1. As you worked on the Debt Document, did you notice if your beliefs have changed about yourself, God, or others since the loss of your loved one to suicide?

2. Spend time looking over the beliefs you're holding now and decide if you want to change or modify them. For example, you may believe the world isn't a safe place anymore because you've lost the sense of security since your loved one died. Be curious if you want to live out your life holding on to that belief. How does it help or limit you moving forward? Do this with each belief you hold.

3. How did it feel to go through the empty chair exercise?

4. How did you feel about this statement? *They never have to make it up to you or pay you back—they are free.* Was it hard to agree with this statement?

5. How will you maintain that attitude with the person(s) you have forgiven?

6. If you were able to complete the exercise and forgive your offenders, did you feel a sense of freedom? Why or why not?

7. What challenges do you foresee with reconciliation and restoration? Why?

Chapter 11

Children: Living Behind the Shadow

"Please reach out. Speak up. The worst thing you could do is to stay silent, like I did for so many years."

—Kelsey Elizabeth Oney[1]

There was a note, but it wasn't found till much later. They were all at school. It seemed like any other normal day, only it wasn't. She remembered it was cold, that kind of bone-chilling cold that penetrates joint and marrow. When they got home, Scarlett could sense there was something terribly wrong. People filled the house. Eventually, a neighbor would take Scarlett and her siblings across the street, but before they left, she remembered the knock at the door and the police coming into their home. She remembered her mother sobbing.

Scarlett felt scared and confused. Later that night, her mother sat them down in the family room and told them. "Your father's dead. He shot himself. That's the end of it." Her mother's hand shook as she dropped the blood-stained wedding ring her father always wore. "My mother only spoke of it that once," Scarlett explained as she recalled the event as an adult, "but she never recovered after finding him. I was ten."

Now, at forty-five, she sat in my office describing the decades of turmoil she had lived through trying to understand, trying to make sense of his suicide. Scarlett had battled her own mental health issues for years, fearing that one day she would probably take her own life like her father had. The years of silence had taken a toll on her.

Losing a parent to any death is never easy for children; but those who have a parent die by suicide are more likely to face adverse outcomes. These can include drug problems, alcohol addiction, relationship problems, depression and anxiety disorders, complicated grief, and for many, a lifelong struggle with suicidality.

Scarlett's experience growing up in silence in the 1970s is unfortunately fairly common. Stigma being what is was then, people didn't think children should be told much. "My mother tried to bury her pain," Scarlett said, crying. "She wanted to erase it all from her memory and ours. We didn't want to ask her about it because we didn't want to cause her more pain, so we tried to go on the best we could, holding it all inside."

Research psychologist Albert Cain has studied parental suicides extensively, and he's identified recurring themes surrounding what he calls "the telling," which is essentially the story given to the child by the surviving parent or guardian.[2] There are a lot of good guidelines to consider about this telling, so let's explore some of them.

WHY WE TELL

How parents should talk to their kids about suicide depends on how old the child is. The key is that parents *do* talk. We often forget that children are people too. They are curious, and they want to know "why" just like we do. Silence only fuels dysfunction.

As we discussed in a previous chapter, your ideas about how to communicate about grief and loss will influence your willingness to talk to your children. Keep those beliefs in mind, and be prepared to modify them as you read through this section, because talking about your loved one's suicide is what will eventually serve your children best, even if you have to allow some time to go by first.

If I was a therapist treating Scarlett and her siblings today, some of my recommendations for talking to children of varying age groups would include the following:

Telling: Children 6–8

Scarlett had a younger sister, Maddy, who was six when their father died. When you're talking to children in this age group, it isn't necessary to go into details. Using the guidelines of the American Academy of Pediatrics, you may not want to tell your child the death was a suicide at this age; but remember, it will always be better for your child to hear truth from you as opposed to someone else. At age six, children are just coming into an understanding that death is final.

Children of Maddy's age won't understand what suicide is. Tell them it's when someone is so sad, they decide to end their life. If the child asks why, you can tell them that when people die by suicide, they aren't healthy and are very, very sad. They felt like living was just too hard and they didn't think anyone could help them feel better. They couldn't see any other way to make the sadness stop.[3] Keep your answers short and concise. Always let the child lead. Check in with your child frequently to see how they're doing emotionally or if they want to talk.

Be guided by your child's questions and what you believe they need to know. Be especially mindful of what they can understand. Keep your answers as simple as possible. Be open to your child's questions and make certain children don't blame themselves in any way. Because children are egocentric, they aren't able to think abstractly, so if something bad happens, they can't reason it out or think someone else may have had some culpability. They blame themselves.

For a child Maddy's age, it would be common for them to think they did or said something that caused the parent to want to die. For instance, they may believe that if somehow they had been a better kid, their parent would have been happier. If they ask if it was their fault, and they may, assure them that they did nothing wrong.

Children in the six to eight age group often use play, art and drawing, and games to express feelings. You can utilize those expressive forms as a springboard to see how they're thinking and feeling. If you see something distressing in their play or art, don't hesitate to get them help from a therapist who specializes in grief/trauma/ suicide counseling for children.

Telling: Children 9–12

An eight-year-old's understanding of death is still fuzzy and often associated with old age and illness. Scarlett was ten when her father died, but she understood more than most kids. By age twelve, children possess an understanding that death is final, but there is no single answer to help kids understand *why* a parent (or other loved one) would want to end their life.

As they get a little older, children will likely have more questions, and not telling them what they want to know will only lead them to speculate and jump to conclusions, some of which may not be true. They also have vivid imaginations, and when they aren't told the truth, they can invent all kinds of stories. Again, don't give more information than a child asks for.[4]

Telling the truth also builds trust with children. They are much smarter than we give them credit for, and they pick up on our non-verbal cues such as trying to hold back tears, worried looks, collapsed posture, and hushed conversations. They know something is wrong. You may want to wait until you are in a better space to talk in-depth about the suicide, since your despair will be evident and children already fear upsetting the parent left behind. I've seen this a lot in my practice with kids and teens, so if you're in process with your own grief, find a therapist your children can talk to.

Suicide can be a scary concept for children of any age, and they often believe that because a parent took their life, they too will end up dying in the same way. If you find they're ruminating on this idea, assure your child it isn't true. If they persist, don't hesitate to get them professional help. Again, make sure you look for a therapist that specializes in trauma/suicide and has experience specifically with your child's age group. (Suggested resources for help are listed at the end of the book.)

Children can also be fearful the parent left behind will die or leave them. They may become clingier (anxiety), have angry outbursts, or act out in some other way. They may exhibit behavioral difficulties at school or regress in some area of their lives. This is especially true of the six-to-eight-year-olds. Assure your kids that you are doing all you can to get the help *you* need and to take care of yourself so you can be there for them.

Tell them not to be afraid if they see you cry or getting upset. Explain that you miss your spouse (or other loved one) and grief is normal. In this way you will encourage your kids to feel free to express their sadness when it comes up. Let them know that although you are deeply sad and life is very hard right now, it won't always be this way. Let them know that if they have questions or need to talk, it won't upset you. Things will get better in time. Don't ever tell them not to cry or be sad.

Telling: Teens 13–18

By adolescence, children know and accept that death is final. They may seek more support from their peers or use friends as a distraction from their grief. They may not be able to put words to their pain, so they need encouragement, help, and support. They may appear to be coping well, but inside they are still hurting.

If the surviving parent is having a difficult time, it's easy to over-look the pain of a child/teen, especially if they seem to be doing okay on the surface. My children were obviously grown and had their own families when my husband died, but I regret I wasn't able to be present for them the way I would have liked to be.

Adolescents are able to think abstractly toward the later teen years and will undoubtedly have more questions and concerns about the particulars surrounding the parent's suicide. Answer their questions as you deem appropriate. At this age, teens may withdraw; they may have difficulty concentrating at school. They may exhibit anger, anxiety, depression, or changes in eating habits or sleep. If these symptoms persist for several weeks, get professional help for your teen.

Teens often see themselves as invincible and immortal. It's hard for them to consider something bad will happen to them. Because their executive learning skills haven't fully developed, that means consequential thinking—the look before you leap idea. This age group can't consider the consequence of their actions before they act. Remember, the pre-frontal cortex doesn't come online until the latter part of the teen years, but the limbic (emotional brain) is running at high speed by the early teens.

If your teen was in any way involved in witnessing the suicide or finding your loved one, get them professional help as soon as possible. Encourage your teens to talk and express their feelings. Listen. Don't assume that because you've all gone through the same tragedy, everyone will think and feel the same way. Grief is unique to each person, so everyone should respect the other person's journey.

If you are not managing your grief or PTS well, a child can sometimes take on an adult role, such as caretaker. They will want to take care of the parent who is left behind. Assure them that you are getting the help you need in order to continue parenting *them*. Emotionally they may struggle with finding meaning and purpose in life.

If your family follows a faith tradition, share your faith with them, but understand that your kids may feel angry at God. Assure them that this is normal. If they're open, talk to them about it, or see if they'd like to talk to a pastor or therapist about their feelings and beliefs. These kids need as much support as possible. Respect their feelings and give them space if they need it.

THE AFTERMATH

Going back to Scarlett's story from the beginning of the chapter, we'll find that she was haunted by many questions and unfinished business for years. In our work together, she was able to process the deep sense of sadness that shrouded her very existence and the longing she had for her father that was never satisfied.

Scarlett had been particularly lonely after the death of her father. She needed her mom, but her mom was so preoccupied with her grief that she was emotionally unavailable for her kids. This is common in families bereaved by suicide. Each person is so enmeshed in their own pain, they are often unable to offer the support others need.

Siblings of the person lost to suicide are particularly at risk for developing complicated grief. Desperate to help their parents through their grief these kids learn to put their needs aside to spare their parents more pain. Many hear the repeated message they need to "be strong" for their parents, which can shut down any expression of their own grief. They can feel neglected and even angry at their sibling for doing what they did to the family.[5]

Siblings face their own problems with stigma. Friends may abandon them, say thoughtless things, or act like the death never happened. Others report ending friendships due to the impatience of others who thought they should be over it by now. Many teens I've counseled have felt they had to pretend everything was okay to avoid feeling awkward around their peers. They tend to isolate themselves out of shame.[6]

While Scarlett didn't lose a sibling, she spent years watching her younger sisters struggle with all the things mentioned above. Group sessions with her sisters revealed a lot of pain and unresolved anger that took a good bit of time to process. Over the next few years, Scarlett's mother dated several men who were not, according to Scarlett, good enough for her. She felt her mom was settling because she was so lonely. Scarlett understood her mother's loneliness as she got older, but she resented the time her mother took away from their family to find love.

Eventually, Scarlett was able to forgive her mother for the years of silence and how that had affected her and her sisters. Once she let go of all the hurt and pain, her depression lifted. She was, in time, ready to move on with her life and put the past behind her. She was beginning to write a new story for herself.

Before her mother died, she handed Scarlett a worn box filled with some of her father's things. In it, Scarlett found the note her dad wrote before he took his life. In the letter he wrote to each of his children and told them how much he loved them. He wanted them to know that it was his own (perceived) failures and sense of purposelessness that caused the spark of life to be distinguished from him. He was tired of the fight. He prayed that when they thought of him, it would be with compassion and mercy. This was a turning point in her healing. She finally had some sense of closure.

I didn't hear from her for several years and then out of the blue she called to tell me she had become a counselor. She wanted to give back, she wanted to help those who struggled with suicidal ideation, and she wanted to work with survivors who had been left behind. Scarlett was paying it forward and redeeming in her own way what had been stolen from her and her family. In the end, she was happy.

EXERCISES

Given the disparity of kids ages in this section, I'll limit my remarks here to things that would be age appropriate for any child or teen while trying to honor their deceased loved one and process their pain.

Plant a tree in honor of your loved one.

Leave a seat at the table on holidays or special occasions to honor your loved one. Go around the table and have each person speak about your loved one if they want to.

Create a collage, paint a picture, or write a poem.
Make a memory box. Help your child choose special items that either belonged to their loved one or held some special

significance. The child can decorate the box themselves or with help.

Make a hope box. In this box, place items that help your child to regain hope that things will get better in time. These items may include Bible verses, a special saying or poem, or an icon or symbol, like a cross or something that belonged to their loved one that may instill hope.

Pick a day to celebrate your loved one's life together as a family. It doesn't have to be the day the person died but make it a positive experience by doing something special, such as going to a place your loved one enjoyed, talking about how your loved one impacted your lives, and reminiscing about fun times together.

Give your child a special memento in remembrance of their loved one. It can be individualized to have special meaning for each child, such as a music box with a song the parent use to sing to the child or something engraved with a special name the child was called. This could be kept in their memory box.

Begin new traditions to honor your loved one.
Read Bible verses on hope and faith.
Write a letter to your loved one.
Write a letter from your loved one to you.
Do a walk for suicide prevention as a family.
Write on a blank piece of paper: "I worry about . . . " or "I am afraid of . . ." and have your child draw a corresponding picture.
Talk to your child about any nightmares they're having.
Draw the dream and then draw an acceptable ending for it.

Consider This

1. If you are the parent(s) of a child who has died by suicide,
   what thoughts do you have now about talking to your other
   children?

2. What activities, if any, have you used with your children to
   memorialize your loved one who died?

3. Have you checked in with your family members to see if they
   want to talk about how they're each doing? Could you make
   that a regular practice?

4. What are the most pressing needs you see in your other
   family members? How might you meet those in the midst of
   your own grief?

5. Have you noticed anyone in the family system who wants to
   be the caretaker of others? If so, who?

6. How can you help that child understand that is not their
   role?

7. How are you ensuring your own care, first, so that you can
   better help your child/children?

Chapter 12

Alongside

*"It's your road, and yours alone. Others may walk it with you,
but no one can walk it for you."*
—ATTRIBUTED TO RUMI[1]

"I will fear no evil, for you are with me."
—PSALM 23:4

"The bravest thing I ever did was continuing my life when I wanted to die."
—ATTRIBUTED TO JULIETTE LEWIS[2]

After Mike died, all I kept saying was I wanted to somehow redeem
the tragedy, to touch one life or prevent one suicide. I would never
have been able to survive, much less help other people, had it not
been for my kids and grandkids walking alongside me, as well as
dear family members and friends, each laying down their lives to
help me in many different ways. I will be forever grateful for their
selflessness, kindness, and empathy.

Each of you reading this book has done so for purposeful and
painful reasons; you are a suicide loss survivor, or you are the loved
one of a suicide loss survivor. If you are the latter, you will have the
difficult task of walking *alongside* the person you love. It will be
messy. It will be painful. It will be exhausting. It will be uncharted
territory because suicide isn't like any other loss.

At times, you'll most likely grow weary. At times, you'll wonder
if your loved one will make it through. Maybe you'll wonder if you'll
make it through. As I reflect back on that first year and a half and
think of those who loved me, lived with me, and cared for me, I realize

what it must have been like for *them,* tending one who was breathing but barely alive.

What does it mean to really walk alongside someone? From my experience, I think the greatest gift I received was, and is, the constantly attuned and compassionate presence of a handful of people who have gone the distance with me. By this I mean, there are a few people I know will always listen, will never grow weary, annoyed, or frustrated with me, and will understand when, after all this time, I'm *still* having a bad day.

They will sympathize with my latest nightmare, let me cry and be angry, or sit and cry with me. They will never tell me to "move on." They will never expect me to "get over it." They will never throw clichés at me, and they will never say, "Well, at least . . ."

They are always available. Always compassionate. Always attuned. Always patient. They praise my perseverance. They acknowledge my sadness. They are always concerned about my mental health and physical well-being. They lift me up when my head is bowed down. They don't baby me. They don't feel sorry for me. And they don't patronize me. They are a literal lifeline for the occasional days that still seem unbearable. Most of all, they see my faith as a living anchor to my healing and they always encourage me to come back to what I know to be true.

This may seem like a tall order for you if you're the one walking alongside a loved one. That's why it's important for there to be several people who can help. It's also important for you, the survivor, not to lean in too heavily to those who are walking alongside. You have to do the work to heal; no one else can do that for you. If, instead, you're reading this book to help your loved one on this most arduous journey, let's look at some of the things that may help *you.*

CONNECTION: THE SOURCE OF EMPATHY

The common denominator of this idea of a *constant* presence is centered around the idea of empathy. Many of us get that word confused with sympathy, so let's take a look at the difference. Both of these traits are strong pillars of emotional intelligence, but they are quite different. Empathy is putting myself in *your* shoes. Empathy creates feelings that drill down on my own soul because of what *you're* going through. It fuels connection. You've heard the saying "I feel your pain"; that's the heart of empathy.

Sympathy is about feeling sorry for someone going through a difficult situation. It doesn't necessarily require a person to feel what another person feels. Empathy is about feeling *with* someone, rather than feeling *for* someone. With sympathy, there's a natural detachment from the situation.

Think back on what you learned from attachment theory (chapter 4). Because attachment theory is about our closest relationships being a secure base and safe haven, it makes sense that if danger occurs, you're going to seek closeness to your attachment figure to feel safe, secure, and calm. You feel what that person feels, and you can use your emotional responses as a way to soothe and calm your significant other.

If you haven't already done so, take a moment to think about this and do what I did above. Make a list of any negative beliefs you may be holding about yourself or any other characters in your story. Set it aside for now, since we'll use it later.

Now imagine this scenario:

You're trapped in another century. You find yourself in a large dark medieval dungeon. It's damp, cold, and dark. Suddenly, you notice a huge dragon coming toward you. You're terrified. You're frozen. You want to run but there is no way to escape.

Then you feel a hand on your shoulder and notice your best friend, spouse, or partner is standing beside you, saying, "It's okay. I'm here. You're not alone." As bad as things are, somehow you feel less terrified. The darkness isn't so black, the dragon isn't as scary, and you're not so alone. This is the heart of attachment. This is the heart of empathy.

Why does it work this way? Because in order to connect and be present with *you*, *I* have to connect with something within myself to feel your pain. This is possible because of mirror neurons. Mirror neurons are at the heart of empathy because when these neurons fire, there is a twofold outcome. They fire when we are performing an action (like crying) and when we see another person performing the same action. This is why we're moved so deeply by watching the characters in a story or a sad movie; because somewhere within their drama, we're connecting to our own sad tale, and we feel empathy for the players on stage. Empathy moves us to action.

With sympathy, we feel bad, but from a distance. We know and acknowledge bad things happen and we feel sorry about it, but what can we really do? Going hand-in-hand with sympathy are those troubling "at least" replies to survivor statements. For example:

"I don't think I can go on without my husband."
"At least you can get remarried."

"I miss my son so much."
"At least you have two other kids to focus on."

"I didn't get to say goodbye."
"At least they found the body, so you can say goodbye now."

Why do we respond this way? Why do we minimize others' pain with these unintentional yet insensitive remarks? Simple. We don't know what to say, so we try to give people a one-liner that will somehow put a cherry on top of a charred cake.

Instead of that approach, try something that will sustain your loved one. Rarely does a one-line response engender healing. Rarely do our efforts to sugarcoat tragedy with a platitude do the trick. The only thing that helps is secure, attuned, and compassionate connection. That's all the survivor needs. To walk alongside means to get your hands dirty. For you, the survivor, the practice of gratitude for those who have and are consistently supporting you is key. Let's take a look.

GRATITUDE: THRIVING TRUMPS SURVIVING

In our discussion on brain science, we learned about the amygdala, the fear center in our brain. Sometimes what happens when we start to heal from the post-traumatic stress of the suicide, the amygdala, which is always scanning the environment for danger, misinterprets our new actions (i.e., going out on a date, exercising, being around people) as being scary and dangerous.

In other words, our brain has gotten used to a certain way of being when we've been in shut-down or hypervigilance mode due to the traumatic experience. When we start behaving differently, acting in ways that exceed what we believe we're capable of, the brain may send us signals that tell us we can't do it. We have to convince our brain that it's okay to try new things and step out in ways that we haven't had the courage to do before. We have to train our brain to, not just to survive, but to thrive.

In his book *Shadow of the Titanic*, Andrew Wilson recounts the stories of survivors of the fateful disaster and how it affected the survivors' life trajectories. Some never recovered; others went on and attempted to thrive. Renee Harris was one of them. She lost her husband, Broadway producer Henry Harris, and went on to become the first woman theater manager and producer in the United States. Renee looked at that night as a defining moment: either she could let herself be consumed by it or try to make her future endurable. She said:

> That fateful night that engulfed me fifty years ago has never entirely disappeared, although it has become buried under the many events that have accrued through the years. There is no doubt in my mind that what I went through that harrowing night in 1912 was a test to find out if I should go through life without my beloved or just give up.[3]

People like Renee Harris didn't have the benefit of all we've learned in the twenty-first century about the brain and trauma and how to heal. In addition to the skills in this book that you've been learning and practicing, you must also allow gratitude in to silence the fears that say "you can't." You can do this by reminding yourself that you're grateful for the things you have accomplished. Even the smallest things you've stretched yourself to do call for a pat on the back.

That may look as small as getting dressed in the morning. In the days following Mike's suicide, just getting up and getting in the shower was a feat, a true accomplishment for the day. I was grateful I could feel the pulsating water on my skin. I was grateful for my friends. I was grateful for my kids and grandchildren. That didn't mean I wanted to go on, but I was grateful, nonetheless. Start small, and tell yourself you *can* do it, and then see if you can. Write about it and how it made you feel.

You will spend plenty of time just trying to survive in the beginning of this journey. Once you make your way out of the wilderness, you'll want to start thinking about what it means for you to thrive. I resented that word for a long time because to me, it meant I was no longer grieving . . . that I was saying *I'm fine, I'm over Mike, so let's move on now.*

If someone said I seemed to be doing much better, I would feel this angry part rising up inside me wanting to scream, "You have NO idea what I'm feeling inside or what I'll live with for the rest of my life!" It wasn't their fault; they were just trying to encourage me. But somehow, for me, it minimized my love and loyalty to Mike. Once I realized I needed to go on for my family, and that God wasn't finished with me, I knew I had to decide what thriving meant for *me.*

I encourage you to do the same because we're all different, and what it meant for me may be totally different for you. No one will ever live in my skin. No one will ever know the depths of my pain in losing my husband. Even though each of us has lost someone to suicide and we can empathize with each other, I can't fully know your pain, nor you mine. We share a common bond, but we are unique in our grief, and we must respect each person's process.

The word *thrive* means to grow or develop, to flourish.[4] I preferred the word "grow" as I moved through my grief journey because it seemed a little more palatable to me, as though I'll always be grieving, but I want to behave in a way that will honor God and give others hope and courage to move forward. Take some time and think about what growing means to you and what that would look like as you make your way through this journey. It will look different as each year passes and as you build sustainable frameworks of meaning for yourself and your family. The key is to reflect and be intentional about your own personal growth.

For me, thriving meant starting to exercise again after six months. It meant starting to date. It meant eating well and getting enough rest. It meant rekindling my passion for my work. Later, it meant remarriage to a fellow widower and a wonderful Christian man.

You can't find meaning and purpose without passion. Ask yourself the questions, "What matters to me moving forward? Who matters to me moving forward?" Start there. Then think of your forward movement as a bullseye and ask yourself what behaviors will get you where you want to go and what behaviors will impair your moving forward.

Take time to survey your life and your behavior. Ask yourself if there is anything that you don't like about how you're dealing with your loss. If that strategy isn't in line with your core values, work on modifying it or eliminating it altogether. Look at your relationships. Perhaps there are people in your life who are dragging you down or causing you to stumble in some way. Maybe there are people who are enabling you. Be honest with yourself and make the necessary adjustments.

The journey toward growth requires mindful reflection. It's realizing that God has placed within each of us qualities that will move us forward if we will simply recognize them and use them.

I believe we've been given everything we need, so let's use it to do something amazing with the time that remains.

WHAT NOT TO SAY: SILENCE CAN BE GOLDEN

All survivors have had things said to them that haven't been helpful or encouraging. Many well-meaning people will say things that will feel devastating to you. They may add additional weight to guilt/shame or make you feel misunderstood. If you're reading this book in the attempt to help a suicide survivor, know that empty platitudes should be avoided. If you don't know what to say, just be still and sit with your loved one. Your loved one doesn't need fixing; they need love and support.

We already discussed stigma and how that affects community reactions to a loss by suicide. Because of this, many survivors won't benefit from support because they will choose not to reveal the cause of their loved one's death. One study revealed that many even lied about the cause of death due to stigma and shame. The telling involves risk, but taking that risk can help destigmatize mental illness and help the individual deal with any shame they're experiencing by actually talking about it.[5]

Here are some common platitudes offered by well-meaning people and the common internal responses of survivors:

"Your loved one is at peace."
That's great, but what about me?

"Your loved one is in a better place now."
That's comforting, but I'm left behind to pick up all the shattered pieces of my life.

"God needed another angel in heaven."
Well, what about me, God, I still needed my loved one! What kind of God are You to take my loved one from me?

"Your loved one isn't suffering anymore."
I'm glad my loved one isn't suffering, but I will have the rest of my life to live and bear this burden.

"Don't worry, you'll get remarried [or have another child, etc.]."
Healing isn't going to be found in replacing my loved one.

"At least you had your loved one for _____ years."
*It doesn't matter how long I've had my loved one, I still wasn't
    ready to lose him/her.*

"I know how you feel."
*You really don't have a clue, even if you've been through something
    difficult, it's not possible to live in someone else's skin.*

"At least they found your loved one's body."
Not worthy of a response.

In addition, if you're trying to comfort a survivor, try to avoid
saying the following:

"You have to move on."
Please allow me to use my own timetable for my grief.

"You seem so much better!"
I just don't show how I really feel. I'm still dying on the inside.

"How long are you going to grieve?"
As long as I need to.

"Your loved one wouldn't want you to be so sad."
*I think my loved one would expect me to miss him/her, and they
    would understand I'd be brokenhearted.*

"Don't cry."
Crying is good for the soul.

What should we say? Here are a few things that are helpful:

I can't begin to imagine how this feels for you, but I'm here if
    you'd like to talk.

You did a great job supporting and loving your loved one till the end.

I'm making a meal; what time shall I bring it?

I'm going to the store, what can I get you?

Do you want to talk, or would you rather be quiet right now?

I'll take you to your appointment.

Can I give you a hug?

Can I pray for you right now?

I'm so sorry you're having a bad day; is there anything I can do that would help?

You did the best you could with your loved one given the circumstances.

I know how much you loved _____. This must be the hardest thing you've ever had to face.

I'll be here for you for as long as it takes.

I've mentioned throughout the book that a support group is vital for a suicide loss survivor. It can be a safe place to share your feelings with people who have actually had a similar experience and know the pain of a suicide loss. They "get it." Sometimes with the longevity of our grief, we can get the feeling other people are tired of hearing us go over and over the same things as we try to make meaning of what happened to our loved one.

That's where a good group comes in. I could always count on my group members to listen and understand my despair. They don't tire of listening because they're going through the same thing. They didn't mind discussing difficult things or seeing me a mess. They didn't judge me or make unhelpful remarks.

I know many of you who are survivors will say, "I don't want to talk about it, it only makes me feel worse. I'm not the kind of person to share my stuff with a group of people." Just be open; even if you don't want to share much in the group, you can learn from listening. It can be also be a place to meet new people and maybe even make a good friend. The worse that can happen is that you go a few times, and if it's really not for you, don't go back.

COMMUNITY

A community is your tribe. The people in your world who know you well enough to want to offer some level of support. Practical things come to mind from my own journey. People brought food, people prayed, people sent cards, people took me to appointments, people called (even if I couldn't talk), and people stopped to visit (some from afar). They didn't give advice, they didn't ask questions, they just sat with me in the darkness.

Some listened when I needed to talk, some cried with me. I'm sure many didn't know what to say, so they said nothing, they just let me take the lead. I was so afraid of being alone, and I needed companions. My dear friend Mary and her husband actually moved in with me while they were building a home in another state.

The community can offer help too. Be on the lookout for services offered in your area such as suicide support groups. Contact the American Foundation for Suicide Prevention or the American Association of Suicidology to see if they provide local groups. Alliance of Hope is a helpful online platform for survivors. Take advantage of these resources to connect with others who are going to understand what you're going through.

If you are a loved one walking alongside someone who has lost a loved one to suicide, you may need to do this research for your friend or family member. They may not be capable right away. They may resist doing much of anything. As I've mentioned, I was traumatized the first year, and my friends took me to appointments and to my group meetings.

There are also suicide walks you can participate in that are

designed to raise money to help with suicide awareness and prevention. I participated in one from a distance in California by having a
poster made of Mike and me and placed on the walk route. It was
a way to honor him. There are local chapters across the country, so
with some research, you can find a chapter that will be a fit for you.
The organization I partnered with for this walk is called the American
Foundation for Suicide Prevention.

The important thing is to use any one of the many suggestions
mentioned throughout the book to give voice and action to your
grief, something that will connect you to your loved one, and your
community.

HOW THE "OTHER HALF" GRIEVES

Grief is a unique process for each individual. That being said, it's no
surprise that after the suicide of a child, couples often have marital
and family problems. Many couples divorce. A contributing factor is
that men and women grieve differently, and that fact is compounded
when the death is a suicide.

To cope, men tend to pour themselves into work. They need to
stay busy and often want to avoid the intensity of their pain. Women,
on the other hand, want to talk about their grief and share their emotions. A woman may feel as if her husband doesn't care, isn't grieving,
or doesn't miss the child that they've lost as much as she does. This
is not true, but it can feel true.

If you are survivors of losing a child to suicide, I encourage you
to get help if you notice that you are disconnecting from your spouse.
Don't wait till things get bad. Statistics on divorce after the death of
a child are high. Don't let yours be one of them.

In the book *Grieving Beyond Gender: Understanding the Ways
Men and Women Mourn*, Kenneth Doka and Terry Martin suggest that men and women express their grief along a continuum of
styles ranging from those that they call *intuitive*, centering on the

expression of affect (emotion), to those they call *instrumental*, which finds expression physically and cognitively.[6]

Men historically lean to the instrumental end of the spectrum—this means they process their losses in isolation, through work, or through fixing. They generally do not seek support in order to process their grief. It's important to be aware of these differences so as not to think your spouse isn't grieving or doesn't care—they do care, they just have different ways of dealing with it. Communication is key here along with respecting what your partner needs.

Men: Understand your wife needs to talk and talk and talk about her pain. Be patient. Listen and empathize with her. Hold her. Cry with her. It's okay to want to be strong for her, but understand she needs to know you miss your child too and you understand her grief.

Women: Understand that your husband needs some solace and alone time. Because men are more left-brain oriented, they want to problem solve and fix. It's hard for them to not be able to fix what has happened and to not be able to fix how you feel; so, also find others who can listen and offer support.

THE FORGOTTEN MOURNERS

Another group of mourners often get lost in the shuffle after a suicide: *siblings*. In the past twenty-five years, "at least 620,000 Americans became sibling survivors of suicide."[7] Often referred to as the forgotten mourners, this group of survivors often experiences complicated grief for a variety of reasons, suffering silently and in the shadows because they don't want to put more of a burden on their already devastated parents.

Michelle Linn-Gust, former president of the American Society for Suicidology, explains the additional loss that siblings often experience:

For those siblings still living at home, they will "lose" their parents for some time as the parents grieve the death of the deceased child. Parents can become so engrossed in their grief that they forget their living children still need reassurance that they are loved and wanted.[8]

If you're a parent and you've lost a child, it's easy to get buried alive in your grief and unintentionally lose focus on what your other children are experiencing. As mentioned, kids will often want to caretake parents after something this horrific happens. Siblings are often told they have to be strong for their parents, adding to their guilt and shame if they need attention.

They also can face a great deal of stigma among their peers, who may think of suicide as cowardly. They may hide their anger, not wanting to give their parents more to deal with. Or they may feel they now have to fulfill expectations they aren't prepared for as a result of the death.

A sibling, whether close or not, represents a deep connection to who a person is, because, for a lengthy period of time, they are *known* by their sibling(s). Even in the craziness of childhood that brings a sense of security. The family history that is shared by siblings creates a strong emotional bond, which when shattered by suicide can make a child feel like an orphan.

If you're older and lose a sibling to suicide and your parents are no longer alive, the tragedy makes you all too aware that you've lost one of your final connections to your family. You may feel sadness that your relationship with your sibling wasn't what you longed for through the years, thereby causing you to regret that you didn't try harder to repair the relationship sooner. These are difficult things to process.

If you weren't close to your sibling, you may not get to share in the decision-making processes after their death. You may not be invited to speak at the service or be acknowledged in the way you wished (or at all). You may feel others are being treated as family and you're on the outside looking in. Others may not understand how important your sibling was to you and because society often minimizes sibling loss, you may not get the emotional support you need.[9] If you're experiencing any of these things, you need to work through your feelings. Talk to someone you trust, or see a therapist to process any grief or anger.

EXERCISES

We've covered a lot of ground in this chapter, so as you look at the following section, feel free to use photographs that are specific to your loss, be it your child, spouse, friend, or family member. If you're doing this with a survivor, just listen as they want to go through pictures and talk about their loved one. Don't try to fix them, just be present.

Phototherapy

After Mike died, I couldn't bring myself to even look at his picture for several months, maybe longer. And yet photographs can be healing because they connect us to the people we've loved. It's funny how an arrangement of simple color pixels frozen in time on paper can drop us right back into moments of happiness or sadness.

I like using photos to help people in the grieving process. As I lecture around the country on suicide, grief, and traumatic loss, I often use movie clips to drive home a point. One I really like is from the Pixar movie *Up*.[10] This animated film tells the story of grief through the point of view of an elderly character named Carl, who has lost his beloved wife, Ellie. This wonderful love story unfolds as Carl reminisces on his life with Ellie through a photo album.

Photographs tell us a story, a story of the heart, and they connect us in powerful ways to those we've loved and lost. When I'm doing this with a client, I ask them (at an appropriate time) to bring in some photos of their loved one and together we go through them.

For this exercise, gather together a few pictures of your loved one. Chose a variety of photos that span time. Keep your journal beside you, and as you look at the photos, begin to write. Note what stirs you as you reflect on the people, places, and things in the photographs.

It's not just about looking at the pictures—it's connecting with them. Try to answer some of the following questions as you view each photo:

1. What story do these pictures tell?
2. What themes come up for you in relation to your loved one?
3. What was good, and what was difficult?
4. How does it feel in your body to experience the emotions the pictures engender?
5. What specific emotions come up as you remember these times with your loved one?
6. What memories do you want to keep tucked away in your heart, and which do you want to forget?
7. What do the photos remind you that you learned from your loved one?
8. What do you see in the photos that keeps you connected to your loved one?

Perhaps you'll decide to make an album that reflects your life together. Ask yourself if it would it be helpful to create a photo album with special pictures. Would this work for you? Why or why not? You may even want to do a scrapbook, using the photos and decorating the pages. You can commemorate things like trips you took, significant life events, or holidays. The point is that this book will tell the story of your life with the person you've lost, embracing all that was good.

Consider This

1. What, if anything, don't you like about how you're dealing with your grief? What can you do about it?

2. If you've lost a child to suicide, have you noticed a difference in how your spouse is grieving? If so, how has that impacted you personally, and how has it affected your marital relationship?

3. If you're grieving the loss of a sibling, do you feel like a forgotten mourner? If so, how? If not, what feels most difficult for you with their loss?

4. Has your grief unintentionally caused you to lose focus and attention on others who are hurting?

5. How has your brain tried to trick you into thinking you can't try new things?

6. What have you done that you're proud of at this point in your journey (joined a group, gone back to church, dated)?

7. How willing are you to join a support group? What do you see as possible benefits to do so? Possible obstacles?

8. Who are the people who are walking alongside you?

9. How are they helping or hindering your grief journey?

10. Who are you grateful for in your life right now?

11. Do you draw strength from the idea that God is with you?
    Why or why not?

Chapter 13

The Time That Remains

"Although the world is full of suffering, it is also full of the overcoming of it."
—HELEN KELLER[1]

The one word that captures how we as suicide loss survivors move forward after such a cataclysmic event is *resilience*. The most common definition of resilience in the past few years is this: *positive adaptation despite adversity.*[2]

Suniya Luthar is co-founder and chief research officer at Authentic Connections and professor emerita at Columbia University's Teachers College. She has called resilience a construct with two distinct dimensions: significant adversity and positive adaptation.[3]

The first construct is a given for the suicide loss survivor—the adversity has been traumatic. The second construct, positive adaptation, is dependent on how the survivor chooses to respond to the pain and how they go about the task of building the muscle of resilience. Growth doesn't just happen, it takes work.

Think about resilience like going to the gym and working out, except that you're not only going to be working out your body, you're going to be working out your mind (which will impact your behavior) to build the muscle of resilience. Brain tissue, like muscle tissue, needs stimulation and exertion or it atrophies. Each time you repeat the same action, you deepen the neurocircuitry for better or worse.

To make sure you understand how this works, let's look at the function of your neurocircuitry. Neurocircuits are groups of neurons that carry out a specific function when activated. Neurons communicate with each other through pathways known as neuronetworks.

Simply put, our cells communicate with each other by firing and then wiring together when a thought or activity is practiced *repeatedly*. That's why your parents probably told you "practice makes perfect" when you were trying to learn a new skill.

Your neurons transmit information to all parts of the body, especially the brain, where this information is stored and interpreted. Remember that the power of changing neuropathways lies in *practice* and *focused prolonged attention*. Neuronets are strengthened with repetition. If we want to promote the growth of new neural pathways, we have to hold the new behavior for about thirty seconds.

Here's a short exercise to try:

If you're working on calming yourself, place one hand on your chest and one on your abdomen. You can also choose to place one hand on your forehead and one hand behind your head. Chose a word to say out loud like "calm." Say it several times over and over until you feel the sensation "calm" brings to your body.

Next, create a peaceful scene in your mind that manifests "calm" in your mind. Now smile. If you feel calm, state out loud that this is your new belief. Your brain will then go to work to process that. Next, move your eyes to the right and then to the left several times. This promotes integration between hemispheres in your brain (if you remember, this is what EMDR does; bilateral brain stimulation).

When the right and left hemispheres are integrated, it locks down the information you've given your brain. You have to intentionally practice this a couple times a day every day to form a new neuropathway. If you don't, all those negative default messages that have become ingrained in your brain will continue because your brain doesn't have anything else to do with them.

Let's be clear. Being resilient doesn't mean that a person isn't subject to psychological or emotional disturbance after adversity.

You wouldn't be human if you didn't experience some kind of disturbance after a traumatic event. The truth is, the road to resilience is paved with peaks and valleys, and a person can show resilience in one aspect of their life, while still struggling in another. Remember, it's not *either/or*; it's *both/and*.

For example, I was struggling with PTSD, depression, and anxiety after the suicide, but I still managed to finish my second book in the process. My publisher graciously pushed back my deadline; but even in my distressed condition, I had times of clarity and I pushed through. I was both struggling and working. I was trying to move forward while still holding the pain.

Why talk about resilience in a chapter titled "the time that remains"? Because in order to move through uncertainty, in order to actually do something productive with the rest of your life, you will need to build the muscle of resilience. The good news is resilience can be taught and learned. Like any other trait you want to develop, you have to practice and be intentional.

After you've lived through losing a loved one to suicide, the level of uncertainty you live with is monumental, and it's normal to want to be able to predict what will happen next because you feel so insecure about the future. It's also normal to predict future outcomes based on what our memory tells us about our *past* experiences. Our mind's reference point to look to the future is colored by the past, so we can easily be swallowed up in a "doom and gloom" mentality, believing that some other bad thing is just around the corner.

Because our sense of security has been annihilated, uncertainty feels even more dangerous. We have to determine to not become smaller versions of our former selves. We can find ourselves feeling paralyzed in the early months because we haven't yet built any new or sustainable frameworks of meaning. If we have to make any major decisions—and many of us have had to—they are made from a tenuous place.

That's why it's important to have significant others walking alongside you during this journey. Trusted family members and friends can lend wisdom and counsel to decisions that need to be made. When we experience being seen, safe, and soothed, we develop an overall felt sense of security and calmness that can carry us through difficult times, leveling the ground to foster a resilient spirit.

WHAT WE KNOW

We've established with certainty that life has its fair share of disruptions and seasons of unpredictability. Bruce Feiler, author of *Life Is in the Transitions*, says that the number of life disruptions we will face in today's culture is growing rapidly. It's not uncommon to see people changing careers, changing religions, or changing locations. Sexuality is in flux, gender confusion is rampant, and many adolescents don't have a clue who they are.

We're also seeing a huge rise in mental health disorders, especially anxiety and depressive disorders and, from 1999 through 2018, the suicide rate increased 35 percent, from 10.5 per 100,000 to 14.2.[4]

Why am I telling you this? Because reading Feiler's work hit me hard. Life's disruptions don't just occur at midlife anymore. Feiler's research statistics are sobering. His data shows that each of us will experience a life disruptor every one or two years; for some people, the disruption will be so big it will cause them to have to reassess who they are and what they want out of life moving forward.[5] That's why building resiliency is so important.

The big question I wanted to answer when I wrote my first book, *Shattered*, was this: are some people born more resilient than others, enabling them to bounce back from extreme "life pileups" as Feiler calls them, or is it something that they've learned along life's journey?

My research revealed several common threads among the individuals I interviewed. First, these folks held a strong belief about the goodness of God in spite of suffering. Second, they were willing to trust again after the adversity. Third, despite the suffering they endured, they were willing to risk opening their hearts again, meaning they were willing to step out and engage with others and the world again. Finally, they were able to forgive in spite of what had happened to them.

For our purposes here, we'll look at some different research that may be helpful for you to develop a more resilient spirit.

RESILIENCE AS A SCIENCE

Are some people born with a greater capacity for resilience? Are they stronger and better able to handle adversity? Or do they just see the world through a more positive lens than others do, making bouncing back a little easier?

In 2012, researchers looked at the psychological factors of individuals who had experienced life changing adversity and measured their genetics, spirituality, social connectedness, and biological factors.[6] Their results showed that genetic factors do have an important influence over our response to stress and trauma. They posit:

> Having multiple genetic, developmental, neurobiological, and/or psychosocial risk factors will increase . . . stress vulnerability, whereas having and enhancing multiple protective factors will increase the likelihood of stress resilience.[7]

That means to foster resilience, we want to focus on strengths (protective factors) and develop them, not focus on weaknesses (risk factors). Regarding resilience, two key concepts are central to the discussion. The first is called *learned helplessness* and was coined by Martin Seligman.[8] If I'm operating under this concept, I believe that I am incapable of changing or controlling my circumstances.

What drives this belief for most people is the repeated "bad luck" or negative experiences that always seem to happen to them. It goes hand and hand with the cognitive distortion of *fortune telling*, where we assume our negative predictions are an already established fact. We want to be aware of this and avoid it.

The other factor, *stress inoculation*, is an adaptive stress response people develop. They become more resilient than would be expected to the negative events of life. Stress inoculation therapy actually prepares people to handle stress by exposing them to it in order to increase their psychological resilience against stressors. It's the old "what doesn't kill you makes you stronger" idea.

As a survivor, you've been exposed to more stress than most people, and if you're reading this book, that tells me you want help to move forward. I came through my experience with the attitude that there isn't much left that would level me. I'm a warrior, and so are you!

Another integral part of Seligman's theory are the three words all starting with the letter P that can help us understand what undermines resilience. They are as follows:

1. Personalization—this means things are always my fault.
2. Pervasiveness—this means my problems will apply to all situations in all domains of my life.
3. Permanence—this means this will always be the case and things will never change.[9]

You'll recall from our cognitive distortions list that *personalization* is seeing everything as being your fault or your responsibility. If you hold this perspective, it makes bouncing back from adversity more difficult. For instance, I personalized Mike's suicide as being my fault.

An example of *pervasiveness* would be seeing something that's happened in your life as affecting every domain in your life negatively (spiritual, physical, emotional, work, family, friends, etc.). Not only was something your fault, but it will be pervasive in all the above-mentioned areas of your life. It goes hand in hand with magnifying and catastrophic thinking. As time goes by, you must begin to acknowledge that bad feelings will ease, and they won't affect every area of your life.

Permanence is believing that bad feelings will last *forever*. Negative situations will not only last forever, but they are also unchangeable.

Holding these negative beliefs can hinder our resilience and make us feel like giving up. We think, *Why bother trying because I'm always going to feel this way, and I'll never recover.*

Again, I felt and believed those things for a long time, but healing began to come when I was able to embrace what did remain: my kids, my grandkids, and my work. They gave me a reason to want to live my fullest life. As bad as you feel right now, I can assure you things will shift as time goes on, and you will actually begin to have some good days.

It's important that you take a look at each of these three "Ps" and your current beliefs about each one. Where you are in your journey will radically impact how you see these three perspectives. They will continue to shift and change as you move through time.

HOW TO DO IT: KEYS TO BUILDING RESILIENCE

To build the muscle of resilience, we know we have to be intentional and practice the skills that grow the muscle. Here are some things to consider to help you move in the right direction. In the previous chapter, I talked about the concept of *alongside* and stressed the importance of relationships in order to heal from adversity.

One of the first things you want to consider in building resilience is *making connections* with empathetic and understanding people. We've already seen that because stigma is such a huge obstacle, many people tend to isolate after a traumatic event. Take the time you need in order to heal, but make connecting a priority. We are wounded in relationships, but we're also healed through relationships.

One way you can do this is by finding a support group or a group in your church. Not only will you forge strong relationships if you get involved, but you'll also find hope for the future, a new life with new friends. Resilient people aren't afraid to ask for help from others when they need it.

Resilience is about developing *strength*, so build it by exercising your body. You don't have to run a marathon, but you need to do something. I tried yoga, and found it very helpful. Research has also shown it to be useful for healing in trauma.[10] Be willing to try something new. Exercise helps with everything, especially managing stress and reenergizing the body following the exhausting experience of grief.

Foster physical and emotional well-being by getting enough rest, eating well, and avoiding the negative pitfalls of masking your pain. We've covered negative thinking a lot in this book so *always be on the lookout for thinking errors and toxic thoughts.* They undermine resilience. You will need to remind yourself that you are not defined by this adversity and you are not helpless. *Self-compassion and an optimistic outlook* foster resilience.

I felt helpless for a long time, especially in areas where I had no experience, like managing our estate. Mike did everything, and so I was thrust into situations I felt totally inadequate to handle. Thankfully, I had my son and some great friends who helped me with financial matters. What is most important is your *response* to whatever you may be facing. You may not know all the answers, but there are people out there who do. Take advantage of their knowledge and ask for help. There is wisdom in counsel.

Resilience is about rewriting your narrative and *creating a healing story.* Donald Meichebaum has written extensively on the topic of resilience. He attributes creating *healing stories* to resilience. He has found that resilient individuals tell coherent stories that create *meaning* out of the stressful life experiences they've gone through. They see themselves as being agents of change (with God's help). When we attribute our growth to personal effort, *self-efficacy* flourishes, another correlate to resilience.

As we've seen, the story you're telling yourself is *everything.* After my mom died, a powerful image came clearly to my mind. I was standing in front of a seemingly endless dirt road. The meaning was obvious: I had to make my way down this long road of grief, and I was scared because a pivotal person in my life was no longer there to guide me. I didn't want do life without her.

I've often seen the same image in my mind with Mike's death, only this time I knew I had to travel the road *alone*. As time has gone by and I've looked back down the years, it's oftentimes been easy to get tangled up in this idea of the "other life" I was supposed to be living. But that's not the life I have now, and when I don't live in the right story, it levels me, and it robs me of the things I am grateful for.

To foster resilience, you'll want to think about being grateful for the story you're living in, even if it feels you don't belong there. Keep asking yourself what really matters to you now. What do you want to do now? Who is important to you now? How will you redeem what happened to you and your family because of your loved one's suicide?

Take time to think about this and set goals accordingly. See, when we're living in the story that is no longer possible, we can't be who we are now, and we can't grow into what we're meant to become, and building that new identity is critical for healing and wholeness. When we're focused on all we've lost, it's hard to be grateful for what we've found, in others and in ourselves.

Make a list of the areas in your life you want to survey (things like your work, relationships, personal growth, recreation, spirituality). Then ask yourself if your behavior is lining up with who you want to be in each of these areas. After you've made your list, take some time to look at your strengths. If you feel you're lacking in any of the areas you wrote about above, ask yourself how you can develop the qualities necessary to be the person you want to be. What barriers will you have to overcome? How will you get back on track or get the necessary support you need if you find yourself falling backwards?

My heart for you is this: that in time, you would be living your fullest and most authentic life possible as you move forward. So, when you're tempted to live in the story that isn't possible anymore, when your soul is screaming out "I don't want this!"—don't deny it or push it away; instead embrace the sadness, allow it to cleanse your tattered soul, and then let it pass. Moving forward doesn't mean you're leaving your loved one behind. That will never happen. But you have to live, and doing so requires moving forward while still holding the pain.

There is no quick fix to any of this. It takes hard work and determination and there won't always be a perfect solution to each obstacle you face, but acknowledge that it's okay. Just remember that whatever steps you're taking, they should be guided by your *core values*. The suffering you have endured will help you identify with others' suffering and stir the desire to *walk alongside them* in their suffering. This is another resilience-building trait: to be selfless and help others in need. In this way, we can take our own pain and turn it into hope by giving of ourselves.

Our success moving forward then, depends on the tools we pull out of the toolbox. What resources do we have, what acquired skills will we put into practice, and how will each of these traits of resilience serve us when the specific demands of life's stressors weigh down on us in the aftermath of the suicide?

THE "IT" FACTOR

In my research on resilience, I was excited to discover that the most significant determinant of this concept boiled down to one thing: the quality of an individual's close personal relationships. Remember, this most notably begins early with parents and caregivers. In every study of resilience over the last fifty years, the concept of "attachment" (which I believe is born out in the idea of "alongside," meaning others walking with us in our journey through grief and suffering) was the best predictor of people learning to bounce back after adversity.[11] Bessel van der Kolk of Boston University School of Medicine says, "How you felt as a child is a great predictor of how you manage all kinds of difficult situations later in life."[12]

At this point in our journey together, I'm sure it's no secret to you that I'm a Christian. Along with great friends and family, my faith has been the "it" factor that's gotten me through this tragedy. I have mentioned that along my path, God did some amazing things to help in my healing. I've shared a couple of them with you, but I'd like to leave you with one more.

If you didn't find your loved one after their death, you've most likely imagined horrible images of the scene. If you did find them, you have an up-close-and-personal horror that you will always carry in your mind. For me, that horror was replaced, I believe, by a God who loves me enough to give me another image to focus on: the cross of Jesus.

For me, the cross symbolizes the promises of God. It reminds me that the hope I have is eternal, and that nothing, not even suicide, is beyond the scope of redemption. The despair I felt over Mike being alone in those last hours as he contemplated suicide and carried out the suicidal act has been eradicated because I know that God was with him (even if Mike couldn't feel it), and that is enough.

Now, when my mind goes back to that horrible day, and it still does from time to time, I can immediately shift my focus to the beautiful image of God beside Mike, and the horror present in that moment is lifted. See, according to author Chris Johnstone, "stories of resilience tend to have turning points where something shifts, new possibilities are opened and unexpected opportunities found."[13]

So, according to the research showing that the closest personal relationships are the most robust predictor of resilience, mine is with my heavenly Father and how He cared for me (and how I know He cared for Mike) through this most devastating and traumatic event. The turning points creating the shifts came for me in all the moments that God showed up and gave me hope. This is the "it" factor that helped catapult me forward and allowed me to demonstrate resiliency.

As you press on, may you take the tools that you found helpful in this book and use them in your journey toward healing. May you be gentle with yourself, giving yourself the gift of time and recognizing that no two journeys through grief are the same. And may you find the strength to author a new story of meaning beyond the ruins and find purpose for yourself and those you love.

EXERCISES

Resiliency Factor Exercise

Using the words listed below, write about how you see yourself (or don't see yourself) demonstrating these inner qualities or strengths. Then, list specific examples of how you have demonstrated that strength during times of adversity. If you don't see that particular word as a strength, write about how you would like to develop the quality and the steps you may need to take to do so.

These questions will help get you thinking. When you've finished writing about the words, record the answers to the questions in your journal.

1. How have you managed to carry on in the face of adversity?
2. How have you kept things from getting worse?
3. What specific inner strengths do you possess that make it possible to carry on?
4. Are these strengths you had before the tragedy, or have you developed them through your journey?
5. What, if anything, hindered you from focusing on your strengths?
6. If this particular trait isn't a strength, do you want to work on developing it? How will you do that?
7. How willing have you been to reach out and ask for support?
8. How much effort have you put into dealing with challenges that have arisen?

Look over this list of words below. Try to write a few words or sentences about each of them in your journal, focusing on how you see yourself demonstrating or not demonstrating each particular trait.

Motivated	Intelligent	Warrior	Responsible
Persevering	Faithful	Communicative	Risk Taker
Determined	Focused	Empathetic	Confident
Strong	Energetic	Idealistic	Patient
Courageous	Spiritual	Integrity	Curious
Optimistic	Grateful	Persistent	Healthy
Sharing Emotion	Connecting	Flexible	Positive

How did it feel to do this exercise? Record your insights. The goal here is not only to have you identify your strengths, but to have you *own* them. That's why I wanted you to *write* out specific situations where you have seen yourself demonstrating any particular character trait. Always ask yourself: *Is this trait connected to my core values, and is it congruent with the person that I want to become after this loss?*

One last thing to think about . . . Look at the diagram below. The word *concern* on the right of diagram stands for all the things in life that affect you—things you may be prone to worry about like work, relationship issues, finances, family. The word *influence* on the left stands only for the things you can personally control; namely, your thoughts, attitudes, actions, and beliefs. That's it.

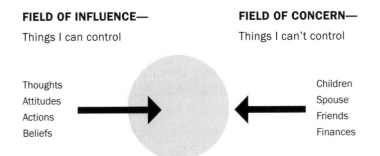

FIELD OF INFLUENCE—   **FIELD OF CONCERN—**

Things I can control   Things I can't control

Thoughts	Children
Attitudes	Spouse
Actions	Friends
Beliefs	Finances

Take a sheet of paper and write down all the things that are in your control from the inside of the diagram and write about how you can personally take action to control the things only you have influence over: your thoughts, attitudes, actions, and beliefs. From the right side of the diagram, record all your concerns. List what your fears and worries are about each area.

Record specific times and situations where you have managed to control those four categories. Ask yourself what action did you take to get yourself to the place you wanted to go. Was it helpful? Were there actions you took and later realized that they were not helpful? If so, what were they, and how will you avoid them in the future? If you can do a positive resilience-based behavior once, you can repeat it. Because of the work you've accomplished thus far, you will have some solid skills to draw from.

Now, think of the things you wrote that aren't under your direct control. Again, list some examples of times when you tried to control a situation or another person. Ask yourself, was there any time where you were able to see that your efforts to control a particular person or a situation were futile, and you decided to surrender control? How did you do it? Remember, surrender doesn't mean we do nothing, it means we change our attitude and *relinquish* our rights to make another person responsible for our well-being.

I did this with Mike. I knew he was depressed, and for a while I kept nagging him to get help or go on medication. He refused to comply, and so I decided that I was not the one who could take responsibility for his mental health and well-being, so I stopped nagging him. At first, I was angry, but then I realized it had to be his decision to get help or it wouldn't work. He finally came around, although it was too late.

We know that nowhere is the uncontrollability of events more evident than for the person who has experienced the suicide of a loved one. In situations like these, life's most extreme moments, the options for personal control are severely limited. It takes a long time to even think clearly after a suicide has occurred, and you may struggle for a what seems like an eternity to control your thoughts and attitudes. Here is where self-compassion comes in. I didn't even start considering any of what I'm telling you now for at least a year and a half.

If you're struggling to surrender control in certain areas, be curious about what's standing in your way now. Generally, it's a fear accompanied by an underlying belief. Surrender means relinquishing unproductive efforts to control what's uncontrollable and shifting our focus to what we have the power to choose. Then you can direct your efforts to problem solving.

You may very well have to confront some negative emotions; but if you are willing to experience them, you will come to learn that you *can* handle whatever feelings you're having using the skills you've learned. The more you cultivate an accepting and willing attitude and the more you sit with the negative feelings and stay present, remembering to focus and calm yourself, the more empowered you will become. Remember too that life will look and feel quite different as time moves on.

Consider This

1. At this point in your journey, do you see yourself as being resilient? If so, how? If not, why not?

2. What is one step you could take today that would move you toward resilience?

3. What is one quality you could focus on to develop your resilience?

4. How does it feel to say out loud that you are an overcomer? Does it give you more energy or less?

5. What would you want people to say about you and about how you have handled this enormous trial in the years to come?

6. What legacy do you want to leave behind for yourself and your loved ones?

7. What would it feel like to surrender that which is uncontrollable? What steps might help you get there? What obstacles stand in your way?

Living a New Story

"The truth is, falling hurts. The dare is to be brave and keep being brave and feel your way back up."
—Brené Brown[1]

The dreams always have the same theme. They still come in the wee hours of the morning, and I wake up in a cold sweat. In the beginning, I dreaded them. Then my feelings shifted and in some twisted way, I looked forward to them to see if I could somehow subconsciously work everything out to have a happier ending than the one I got. Sometimes I'd succumb to the pull of despair, put the covers over my head, and try to keep the dream going, making up my own happy ending.

The dreams always create a longing, a longing for what once was and can never be again. It's all so very sad. I'm always trying to be with Mike, but it never works out. I always figured it was because of the nature of the death; we all know by now that suicide leaves lots of loose ends. But through the years, as I've been curious about it all, I've realized it's not that. The reason I now believe my nightmares have been such a struggle is because I was living in the *wrong* story.

As a Christian, I have the assurance I will be with Mike again. Without that comfort I would never have been able to go on. But the reality is that I have a long road ahead to live life without him. Obviously, I can't control my dreams, nor the reality of what happened, but if I allowed myself to stay in the story that my dreams continue to perpetuate, I'll drown all over again.

As we've seen, survivors don't want to move on for lots of reasons. We can't even imagine existing in a world without our loved one in it. We feel like we're betraying our loved one; we believe we're incapable of going on without the security they provide us; we think we're being disloyal. We feel guilt, maybe even shame.

But at some point, we have to decide if we want to get back in the game and how that's going to look. We can choose to sit on the sidelines for the rest of our lives; but in the end, will that make us proud of the life we've lived?

Courage isn't the absence of fear, it's being scared to death and moving forward anyway. That's where deciding comes in. Sure, none of us signed up for any of this, but here we are. If we move away from the safety of the sidelines, we know we're going to get tackled, but playing it safe is never the best alternative to heal a heart. Why? Because we lose part of ourselves, and once we do, it's hard to get it back. The longer time goes by, it becomes almost impossible.

I decided on that day I broke down at my daughter's house that I had to be brave. Once you make that decision, you can't take it back if you're really serious. Anything else feels cheap. Mike's words would echo in my mind; "You're the strong one Rita, not me." I never believed it. I never had the chance to own it because I always relied on him. That was the story I was still telling myself; that I couldn't live without him. I wasn't brave enough. That wasn't true.

In the beginning, I stayed alive for the kids. But as the years went on, I began to find my footing again. What I did was find myself. My hopes. My dreams. My passions. I realized there was more work for me to do, and until that was finished, I needed to keep moving. I knew that's what Mike would want me to do—for myself and for our family.

I knew how I wanted to be seen through this tragedy—as a person who showed good courage, who stayed the course and finished strong, who kept the faith. These concepts were all things that reflected my core values and my faith. It will be the same for you. So, think about your story. Honor those in the past who have shaped it and consider who the characters will be as your new story takes shape.

You get to decide what happens next. It doesn't mean that you won't have bad days. It doesn't mean that you won't miss your loved one terribly. It doesn't mean that some days you'll be sick and tired of being brave. It doesn't even mean you'll make all the right choices. It just means you're moving. You're breathing. You're fighting, and you won't give up. One day, you'll realize that the greatest thing you ever did was continuing to press on when all you wanted to do was die. Take the time that remains and use it wisely.

Love the people in your life that matter. Spend time with them, for no day is guaranteed. As suicide loss survivors, we know that all too well. In the blink of an eye everything changes. You wake up one morning thinking your life is predictable and stable and by nightfall it's in ruins.

I wish I could reach through the pages of this book and hug each and every one of you who are reading it. I pray that perhaps one thing in this book helps you to push forward for just one more moment, one more day. I pray that over time, the road before you will widen so that you may embrace the cherished memories of your loved one, along with the pain that only you can touch.

You are survivors. You are heroes. You are warriors. May the Lord bless you and keep you as you make your way out of the darkness and into the light.

Appendix

DEBT DOCUMENT

OFFENDER _____ DATE _____

WHAT HAPPENED	WHAT I FELT/ WHAT I BELIEVED	WHAT I EXPECTED _____

TOXIC THOUGHT RECORD

PAST HURT	FEAR(S)	SITUATION	BELIEFS	FEELINGS	THINKING ERROR

Resources

WEBSITES

Alliance of Hope: https://allianceofhope.org

American Association of Christian Counselors: www.aacc.net

The American Association of Suicidology (AAS) offers a variety of resources and programs to survivors in an attempt to lessen the pain as they travel their special path of grief. www.suicidology.org

American Foundation for Suicide Prevention: https://afsp.org

Center for Suicide Prevention: https://www.suicideinfo.ca/ resource/support-group-for-suicide-survivors

Focus on the Family 1-855-771-HELP (4357): https://www .focusonthefamily.com/get-help/counseling-services-and-referrals

National Suicide Prevention Lifeline 1-800-273-8255: https:// suicidepreventionlifeline.org

Parents of Suicides (POS) and Friends and Families of Suicides (FFOS): https://www.pos-ffos.com

SAVE (Suicide Awareness Voices of Education): https:// save.org/find-help/coping-with-loss

Suicide Awareness Voices of Education: https://save.org/ what-we-do/grief-support/find-a-support-group

TAPS (Tragedy Assistance Program for Survivors): TAPS
Institute for Hope and Healing® is located at TAPS
Headquarters, 3033 Wilson Blvd., Third Floor, Arlington,
VA 22201; https://www.taps.org/suicidepostvention or
call 800-959-8277

BOOKS

Albert Y. Hsu, *Grieving a Suicide: A Loved One's Search for Comfort, Answers, and Hope* (Downers Grove, IL: InterVarsity Press, 2002).

Megan Devine , *It's OK That You're Not OK: Meeting Grief and Loss in a Culture That Doesn't Understand* (Boulder, CO: Sounds True, 2017).

Brook Noel and Pamela D. Blair, *I Wasn't Ready to Say Goodbye: Surviving, Coping and Healing After the Sudden Death of a Loved One* (Naperville, IL: Sourcebooks, 2008).

Acknowledgments

I'd like to acknowledge my amazing acquisitions editor, Amy Simpson. This book wouldn't have been possible without you. Thank you, dear Amy, for believing in this project and for believing that I was the one to write about it. My original title for this work was *Alongside* because I wanted to honor not only the people who walked with me through this wilderness journey and helped me heal, but the idea that healing is only realized through the power of *presence*. Research has borne out this idea for decades now, and I have been blessed through this horrible tragedy to have experienced healing firsthand.

I would also like to thank all the wonderful people at Moody Publishers, especially Amanda Cleary Eastep. I am so grateful for all you poured into this book. It has been an honor and a privilege to work with you through this project.

To my amazing children, Ashley and Michael, you were the reason to keep living, to pass to you both the torch your dad and I lit for you. I'm so deeply sorry you have had to walk such a difficult journey at such young ages. Thank you for standing with me through this dark night of the soul and using your love to literally bring me back to life after losing your father.

To Alex and Ida and for all my beautiful grandchildren, you were all a reason to live when some days all I could see was the blinding darkness.

For my Schulte family: Honor, Tori, Jennifer, and Heather. Thank you for encouraging me, continuing to love me, and never judging me.

For Patty Jo Diamond, my assistant and sister, who still to this day never wearies of listening if I'm having a bad day. You have laid your life down for me in ways I will never forget. There are too many to name. For all you and Greg did for me, thank you with all my heart. It will only be in eternity that so great a sacrifice can be rewarded.

To Mary and Joe, I know you saw things that shook you to the core as you watched post-traumatic stress overcome me. I will never be able to put into words how grateful I am for what you did for me and how much I love you. Your presence that first year saved my life.

For my friends Debbie and Ernie, Donna, Shanda, Tricia, Darrell and Karen, Gail and Warren, Ann and Bill, my widows groups ladies, the women at Mike's office, and for all those I barely knew who prayed for me and stood in the gap, I have seen Christ through every one of you.

For you the reader, I want to acknowledge your bravery for pushing through what you have experienced. Suicide is like no other loss, and I hoped to explain the nuances of that in this book. This is a wilderness journey, and you will be worn threadbare. If you are at the beginning stages of this traumatic loss and are reading this, you will believe your life has been totally ruined. I get that. My heart for you is that as time passes, you will begin to see a bigger purpose for your life beyond the ruins of loss by suicide. I simply ask you to consider this simple question: what do you want *your* legacy to be? If you had an answer, or you're still uncertain, then I pray that through the pages of this book you not only find hope, but you find a meaning and purpose for your life beyond the ruins.

For my Alan, God has been so good to allow two grieving people who had lost their spouses to find each other and bring love, hope, and new life to what was ruined. You made me laugh again, and I will be forever grateful for your love and constant care.

Notes

CHAPTER 1: FALLOUT

1. Anne-Grace Scheinin quoted in Douglas Connelly's *After Life: What the Bible Really Says* (Downers Grove, IL: InterVarsity Press, 1995), 55.
2. Lindsey Lanquist, "WHO: Depression Is the Leading Cause of Disability Worldwide," March 31, 2017, https://www.self.com/story/who-depression-disability.
3. "Secret in Their Eyes," written and directed by Billy Ray, STX Entertainment, 2015, https://www.imdb.com/title/tt1741273/?ref_=ttco_co_tt.
4. M. K. Nock, I. Hwang, N. A. Sampson, and R. C. Kessler, "Mental Disorders, Comorbidity and Suicidal Behavior: Results from the National Comorbidity Survey Replication," *Molecular Psychology*, March 31, 2009, https://www.ncbi.nlm.nih.gov/pmc/articles/PMC2889009.

CHAPTER 2: MAKING SENSE OF THE DESIRE TO DIE

1. "Christie Chubbuck—biography," SSRI Stories, July 15, 1974, https://ssristories.org/christine-chubbuck-biography-fampeople-com.
2. Thomas E. Joiner, "2011 Suicide Prevention Conference: 'Myths about Suicide'" (video), Goodreads.com, https://www.goodreads.com/videos/57138-2011-suicide-prevention-conference-myths-about-suicide.
3. Valerie Rubin, "Tragic TV Drama Unfolds before Unbelieving Eyes," *Sarasota Herald-Tribune*, July 16, 1974.
4. Joiner, "2011 Suicide Prevention Conference: 'Myths about Suicide.'"

5. Thomas Joiner, *Why People Die by Suicide* (Cambridge, MA: Harvard University Press, 2005), 92.

6. WHY PEOPLE DIE BY SUICIDE by Thomas Joiner, Cambridge, MA: Harvard University Press, Copyright © 2005 by the President and Fellows of Harvard College. All rights reserved. Used by permission.

7. "Most Powerful Speech by Man Who Survived Jump from Golden Gate Bridge | Kevin Hines | Goalcast," February 13, 2019, (video), YouTube, https://www.youtube.com/watch?v=HEFBtaOySl8.

8. Thomas Joiner, "The Interpersonal-Psychological Theory of Suicidal Behavior: Current Empirical Status," Science Briefs, American Psychological Association, June 2009, https://www.apa.org/science/about/psa/2009/06/sci-brief.

9. Rita A. Schulte, *Shattered: Finding Hope and Healing through the Losses of Life* (Abilene, TX: Leafwood Publishers, 2013), 14.

CHAPTER 3: THE SILENT SCREAM

1. Edwin S. Shneidman, *Autopsy of a Suicidal Mind* (New York: Oxford University Press, 2004), 162.

2. Carla Fine, *No Time to Say Goodbye: Surviving the Suicide of a Loved One* (Portland, OR: Broadway Books, 1997), 36.

3. A. Pitman, et al., "Effects of Suicide Bereavement on Mental Health and Suicide Risk," *Lancet Psychiatry*, 2014, 1:86–94.

4. "Neuroscience/Neurobiology," Mind Brain Behavior, Harvard University, https://mbb.harvard.edu/pages/undergraduate-tracks-neurobiology.

5. "The Amygdala and Emotions," Effective Mind Control, updated on October 19, 2015, https://www.effective-mind-control.com/amygdala.html.

6. Trevor Hughes, "For Columbine Survivors, Life Is about Finding 'That New Normal' 20 Years Later," *USA Today*, April 20, 2019, https://www.yahoo.com/news/columbine-survivors-life-finding-apos-163213544.html?.tsrc=fauxdal.

7. Ibid.

8. Barbara Monroe developed the "Balls and Jars" concept as an expansion of the work of Lois Tonkin. Lois Tonkin, Cert Counselling (NZ), "Growing around Grief—Another Way of Looking at Grief and Recovery," *Bereavement Care* 15, no. 1 (1996), https://doi.org/10.1080/02682629608657376.

CHAPTER 4: THE MIND-BODY CONNECTION

1. This is a popular inspirational quote, although it doesn't appear to be attributed to any one author.
2. "Take a Deep Breath," American Institute of Stress, August 10, 2012, http://www.stress.org/take-a-deep-breath.
3. From the book Resilience. Copyright © 2018 by Linda Graham. Reprinted with permission by New World Library, Novato, CA. www.newworldlibrary.com, 37.
4. From the book Resilience. Copyright © 2018 by Linda Graham. Reprinted with permission by New World Library, Novato, CA. www.newworldlibrary.com, 46–47.
5. Schulte, *Shattered: Finding Hope and Healing Through the Losses of Life*, 39.

CHAPTER 5: MAKING MEANING

1. Quote from "Love Beyond Stars" Facebook page, https://www.facebook.com/lovebeyondstars2015.
2. Isaac Sakinofsky, "The Aftermath of Suicide: Managing Survivors' Bereavement," *Canadian Journal of Psychiatry* 52, 6 Suppl 1 (2007): 129S–136S.
3. Albert Y. Hsu, *Grieving a Suicide: A Loved One's Search for Comfort, Answers, and Hope* (Downers Grove, IL: InterVarisity Press, 2017), 10.
4. Stephen Joseph, *What Doesn't Kill Us: The New Psychology of Posttraumatic Growth* (New York: Basic Books, 2013), "Introduction: Nietzsche's Dictum," xvii.
5. Anke Ehlers and David Clark, "A Cognitive Model of Posttraumatic Disorder," *Behaviour Research and Therapy* 38, no. 4 (April 2000): 319–45, https://www.sciencedirect.com/science/article/abs/pii/S0005796799001230.

6. Trauma Recovery, "What is EMDR?" https://www.emdrhap.org/content/what-is-emdr.

7. If you are having difficulty with traumatic memories that won't abate, or if you're struggling with shame and guilt and are interested in EMDR therapy, do your research in order to find an experienced therapist who practices this treatment.

8. I first heard the term "remembered resource" during a presentation by Lisa Ferentz, founder of the Ferentz Institute. In an email communication to me, Lisa explained that she was drawing from a workshop exercise led by psychotherapist Babette Rothschild. I then added the word "person" to create the Remembered Resource Person (RRP).

9. "Why Shame and Guilt are Functional for Mental Health," *Positive Psychology*, October 31, 2020, https://positivepsychology.com/shame-guilt/.

10. Jeffrey Jackson, "SOS: Handbook for Survivors of Suicide" (Washington, DC: American Association of Suicidology, 2004), 19.

11. This concept is similar to the jars of grief. In my work with patients, I often draw a pie shape with the focus being to grow certain parts of the self. The jars exercise focuses on the intensity of the grief and how to move on while still honoring your loved one.

CHAPTER 6: STIGMA

1. "What's So Funny about Mental Illness? | Ruby Wax," TED, October 10, 2012, YouTube, https://www.youtube.com/watch?v=mbbMLOZjUYI.

2. Mary Catherine McDonald, Marissa Brandt, and Robyn Bluhm, "From Shell-Shock to PTSD, a Century of Invisible War Trauma," PBS News Hour, November 11, 2018, https://www.pbs.org/newshour/nation/from-shell-shock-to-ptsd-a-century-of-invisible-war-trauma.

3. Ibid.

4. Abram Kardiner, "The Traumatic Neuroses of War" (Washington, DC: National Research Council, 1941), Committee on Problems of Neurotic Behavior, OCLC 123390571. Also see The Conversation: https://theconversation.com/from-shell-shock-to-ptsd-a-century-of-invisible-war-trauma-74911.

5. Suicide Prevention Information: National Veteran Suicide Prevention Report, https://www.mentalhealth.va.gov/docs/data-sheets/2020/2020-National-Veteran-Suicide-Prevention-Annual-Report-11-2020-508.pdf and Resources, http://dphhs.mt.gov/amdd/Suicide.aspx.2020.

6. Sarah Keller, Vanessa McNeill, Joy Honea, and Lani Paulson Miller, "A Look at Culture and Stigma of Suicide: Textual Analysis of Community Theatre Performances," *International Journal of Environmental Research and Public Health* 16, no. 3 (2019): 352, https://doi.org/10.3390/ijerph16030352.

7. Nicolas Rüsch, Patrick W. Corrigan, Karina Powell, Anita Rajah, Manfred Olschewski, Sandra Wilkniss, Karen Batia, "A Stress-Coping Model of Mental Illness Stigma: II. Emotional Stress Responses, Coping Behavior and Outcome," *Schizophrenia Research* 110, nos. 1–3 (2009): 65–71.

8. Ibid.

9. Ibid.

10. Ibid.

11. Franz Hanschmidt, et al, "The Stigma of Suicide Survivorship and Related Consequences—A Systematic Review," *PLOS ONE* 11, no. 9 (2016): e0162688, doi:10.1371/journal.pone.0162688.

12. Sarah Keller, Vanessa McNeill, Joy Honea, and Lani Paulson Miller, "A Look at Culture and Stigma of Suicide: Textual Analysis of Community Theatre Performances," https://www.mdpi.com/1660-4601/16/3/352/htm.

13. Candida Moss, "The Catholic Church's Own Complicated History with Suicide," *The Daily Beast*, December 23, 2018, https://www.thedailybeast.com/the-catholic-churchs-own-complicated-history-with-suicide.

14. Ibid.

15. Natalie Ford, American Association of Christian Counselors World Conference, Nashville, Tennessee, 2017.

16. Kay Warren, "Kay Warren Says 'Don't Tell Grievers to Move On' as 1 Year Anniversary of Son's Suicide Approaches," Facebook post. Used by permission.

CHAPTER 7: EXISTENTIAL SHATTERING

1. This quote is often attributed to Winston Churchill, although there is not definitive evidence he ever stated this. See https:// quoteinvestigator.com/2014/09/14/keep-going.

2. Louis Hoffman and Lisa Vallejos, "Existential Shattering," in *Encyclopedia of Psychology and Religion*, ed. David A. Leeming (Berlin, Heidelberg: Springer, 2019), https://doi.org/10.1007/978-3-642-27771-9_200193-1.

3. Lisa M. Vallejos, "Shattered: A Heuristic Self-Search Inquiry of One Mother's Journey to Wholeness after a Child's Diagnosis of a Potentially Fatal Congenital Heart Defect" (PhD diss., Saybrook University, 2015), 6, quoted in ibid.

4. Hoffman and Vellejos, "Existential Shattering."

5. Louis Hoffman, Heatherlyn P. Cleare-Hoffman, and Lisa Vallejos, "Existential Issues in Trauma: Implications for Assessment and Treatment," August 2013, http://dx.doi.org/10.13140/RG.2.1.5166.2881.

6. Ibid.

7. Aaron T. Beck, A. John Rush, Brain F. Shaw, and Gary Emery, *Cognitive Therapy of Depression* (New York: Guilford Press, 1979), 78.

8. From *What Doesn't Kill Us* by Dr. Steven Joseph, copyright © 2011, 2013. Reprinted by permission of Basic Books, an imprint of Hachette Book Group, Inc.

9. Adapted from *Cognitive Behavior Therapy: Basics and Beyond* (3rd ed.) by John Beck (New York: Guilford Press, 2020), 216. Used with permission.

CHAPTER 8: UNFINISHED BUSINESS

1. *God's Not Dead* (film), written by Hunter Dennis, Chuck Konzelman, and Cary Solomon, 2014, https://www.imdb.com/title/tt2528814/plotsummary.

2. The American Colony in Jerusalem, Library of Congress, https://www.loc.gov/exhibits/americancolony/amcolony-family.html.

3. Albert Y. Hsu, *Grieving a Suicide: A Loved One's Search for Comfort, Answers, and Hope* (Downers Grove, IL: InterVarsity Press, 2017), 102–103, Kindle.

4. Ibid, 107.

CHAPTER 9: MAKING PEACE WITH OURSELVES

1. Kristen Neff and Christopher Germer, *The Mindful Self-Compassion Workbook: A Proven Way to Accept Yourself, Build Inner Strength, and Thrive* (New York: Guilford Press, 2018), 35.
2. Thomas William Herringshaw, *Herringshaw's Encyclopedia of American Biography of the Nineteenth Century* (1898), 132.
3. Neff and Germer, *The Mindful Self-Compassion Workbook*, 35.
4. Ibid.
5. Ibid.
6. "Evolution of The Internal Family Systems Model By Dr. Richard Schwartz, Ph. D.," IFS Institute, https://ifs-institute.com.
7. Kristin Neff, "Self-compassion," https://self-compassion.org/what-self-compassion-is-not-2.
8. Ibid.
9. https://self-compassion.org/wp-content/uploads/2017/08/The_5_Myths_of_Self-Compassion.Psychotherapy.Networker.Sept_.2015.pdf.

CHAPTER 10: FACING THE DARK SIDE

1. Empty Chair Technique developed by Fritz Perls, https://www.mentalhelp.net/blogs/gestalt-therapy-the-empty-chair-technique.
2. Fritz Perls, Gestalt Therapy Verbatim, 1969 reprinted by the estate of Frederick Perls, M.D. *The Gestalt Journal Press*, Inc. A Division of: the Center for Gestalt Development, Gouldsboro, ME, 146.

CHAPTER 11: CHILDREN: LIVING BEHIND THE SHADOW

1. https://themighty.com/2015/09/messages-for-anyone-who-lost-a-loved-one-to-suicide/.
2. https://aeon.co/essays/when-a-parent-dies-by-suicide-how-are-the-children-told.
3. When a Parent Dies by Suicide, https://www.camh.ca/en/health-info/guides-and-publications/when-a-parent-dies-by -suicide.

4. A.S. Rakic (1992). Sibling survivors of adolescent suicide (Doctoral dissertation). Available from ProQuest Dissertations and Theses Full Text database. (UMI No. 304032612), 2.

5. https://my.clevelandclinic.org/ccf/media/Files/bereavement/ understanding-death-grief-mourning-resources-manual.pdf. This is an adaptation of an article by Kenneth Doka appearing in *Children Mourning, Mourning Children* published by Hospice Foundation of America, 1995. Reference: Helping Children Understand Death. Cooperative Extensions Service, Ohio State University.

6. Leah Royden, "Sibling Suicide Survivors: The 'Forgotten Mourners,'" *The Mourning After* (blog), Psychology Today, February 15, 2019, https://www.psychologytoday.com/us/blog/the-mourning-after/ 201902/sibling-suicide-survivors-the-forgotten-mourners.

CHAPTER 12: ALONGSIDE

1. https://www.goodreads.com/quotes/1134640-it-s-your-road-and-yours-alone-others-may-walk-it.

2. https://www.goodreads.com/quotes/854702-the-bravest-thing-i-ever-did-was-continuing-my-life.

3. Andrew Wilson, *Shadow of the Titanic: The Extraordinary Stories of Those Who Survived* (New York: Atria Books, 2011), 323, Kindle.

4. Eve Griffin and Elaine Mcmahon, "Suicide Bereavement Support: A Literature Review," 2019, https://www.researchgate.net/publication/ 333104296_Suicide_Bereavement_Support_A_Literature_Review.

5. https://www.health.harvard.edu/newsletter_article/ supporting-survivors-of-suicide-loss.

6. Kenneth Doka and Terry Martin, *Grieving Beyond Gender: Understanding the Ways Men and Women Mourn*, 2nd ed., (New York: Rutledge, 2010). https://www.researchgate.net/publication/ 51500219_Grieving_Beyond_Gender_Understanding_the_Ways_ Men_and_Women_Mourn_by_K_J_Doka_T_L_Martin.

7. Michelle Linn-Gust, PhD. "Sibling Survivors of Suicide." Legacy Connect. http://connect.legacy.com/inspire/sibling-survivors-of-suicide.

8. Ibid.

9. Ibid.

10. *Up* (film), written by Bob Peterson and Pete Docter, Pixar Animation Studios, 2009.

CHAPTER 13: THE TIME THAT REMAINS

1. Helen Keller, *The World I Live In and Optimism: A Collection of Essays* (Mineola, NY: Dover Books, 2010), 89.
2. S. S. Luthar, "Resilience in development: A synthesis of research across five decades," In D. Cicchetti & D. J. Cohen, eds., *Developmental Psychopathology*, Vol. 3: Risk, disorder, and adaptation, 2nd ed. (Hoboken, NJ: Wiley, 2006) 739-95. Also https://www.ncbi.nlm.nih.gov/pmc/articles/PMC2956753.
3. Ibid.
4. https://www.cdc.gov/nchs/products/databriefs/db362.htm.
5. Bruce Feiler, "How to Master Change," Psychology Today, April 23, 2020, last reviewed July 14, 2020, https://www.psychologytoday.com/us/articles/202004/how-master-change.
6. Steven M. Southwick and Dennis S. Charney, "The Science of Resilience: Implications for the Prevention and Treatment of Depression," *Science* 338, no. 6103 (October 5, 2012): 79–82.
7. Ibid.
8. Martin E. P. Seligman, *Learned Optimism: How to Change Your Mind and Your Life* (New York: Vintage Books, 2006), 44–51.
9. Ibid.
10. Linda Sparrowe, "Transcending Trauma: How Yoga Heals," Yoga International, https://yogainternational.com/article/view/transcending-trauma-how-yoga-heals.
11. Eilene Zimmerman, "What Makes Some People More Resilient Than Others," published June 18, 2020, updated June 21, 2020, *New York Times*, https://www.nytimes.com/2020/06/18/health/resilience-relationships-trauma.html.
12. Ibid.
13. Chris Johnstone, "Inspiring Stories of Resilience," *Positive News*, February 16, 2015, https://www.positive.news/perspective/blogs/positive-psychology-blogs/inspiring-stories-resilience.

EPILOGUE: LIVING A NEW STORY

1. Brené Brown, *Rising Strong* (New York: Penguin Random House, 2017), xvi.

BLOCK OUT THE NOISE THAT DESTROYS AND FIND YOUR ONE TRUE VOICE.

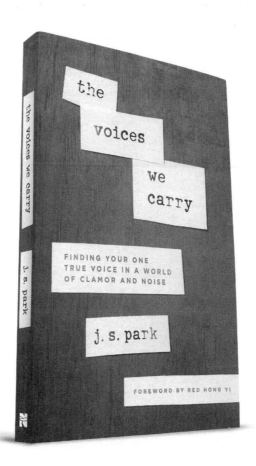

The Voices Model helps you find your one true voice. J. S. Park identifies the false voices we listen to as four inner and four outer voices. In *The Voices We Carry* you'll learn how to identify and silence these voices so you can grow fully and freely.

978-0-8024-1989-7 | also available as eBook and audiobook

You didn't ask for big change, but it happened.
How will you become better because of it?